QUENCHING *the* DIVINE THIRST

Books by Elizabeth Hoekstra

Be Still

A Heart After God

Quenching the Divine Thirst

QUENCHING *the* DIVINE THIRST

ELIZABETH M. HOEKSTRA

BETHANYHOUSE
MINNEAPOLIS, MINNESOTA

Published by Bethany House Publishers
A Ministry of Bethany Fellowship International
11400 Hampshire Avenue South
Bloomington, Minnesota 55438
www.bethanyhouse.com

Printed in the United States of America by
Bethany Press International, Bloomington, Minnesota 55438

Library of Congress Cataloging-in-Publication Data

Hoekstra, Elizabeth M., 1962-
   Quenching the divine thirst : nourishing an insatiable desire for God / by Elizabeth M. Hoekstra.
      p. cm.
   ISBN 0-7642-2549-9 (pbk.)
   1. Spiritual life—Christianity. I. Title.
BV4501.3 .H65   2003
248.4—dc21   2002152597

To any who truly
"hunger and thirst for righteousness"
(Matthew 5:6)

May your thirst be quenched.

ELIZABETH M. HOEKSTRA founded Sweetwater Ministries (formerly Direct Path Ministries) in 1997. Through the written and spoken word her work equips Christians to take their next step toward Christ. Her desire is to see "the body of Christ built up until we reach unity . . ." (Ephesians 4:12–13). This is her eleventh book. She and her family make their home in New Hampshire. For information about Sweetwater Ministries or to contact Hoekstra please visit her Web site at *sweetwaterministries.org.*

ACKNOWLEDGMENTS

At the top of my list of people to thank is my friend first, editor second, Steve Laube, editorial director, nonfiction, Bethany House Publishers, for helping me to recognize my own thirst for God and encouraging me to write to this common need in other people's lives.

To Julie Smith, managing editor, Bethany House Publishers, a special thanks for a light touch with her red pen and her kind words of encouragement throughout the editing process.

Thank you to my writers' group, who for five years have listened to a spectrum of my work from good to terrible and have faithfully come up with gentle challenges and loads of encouragement.

My deepest heart-thanks to my family: Peter, my rock; Geneva, my helper; and Jordan, my hero.

CONTENTS

INTRODUCTION

I 'll keep this short. Because if you are thirsting for a more fulfilling love-relationship with the Lord, you won't want to waste any time before dipping into His well of Living Water. My prayer is that you will find refreshment for your soul and satisfaction for your thirst in these pages.

It's not coincidence that much of Christ's ministry on earth involved water: He was baptized in water. He changed it to sparkling wine. He walked on a lake. He told the waves to be still. He changed people's lives next to water. Some of His disciples made their living fishing on the sea. He washed His disciples' feet in water. And it poured from His side when He was crucified. What better way for us to quench our thirst for Him than to spend time considering parallels between some of these encounters and our lives.

Quenching the Divine Thirst is divided into four parts. Each part highlights a particular event in Christ's ministry involving water. Part One: Come to the Water focuses on the Samaritan woman's conversion at Jacob's well. Part Two: Reflect on the Water is based on an invalid's healing at the pool of Bethesda.

Part Three: Partake of the Water considers Christ's first miracle when He changed water to wine at a wedding banquet. And Part Four: Living on the Water discusses Christ's water-walking miracle.

I've known thirst. I've thirsted for a more satisfying understanding of the "things of God," which is likely the reason you, too, have chosen this book. I've learned there is a tri-part approach to pulling His cup near for a refreshing drink. You'll find these three recurrent themes woven throughout the following pages: revival of your first-love relationship with Jesus Christ, encouragement to get into God's Word to better know His character, and revelation to live a heavenly directed life for His kingdom through obedience to Him. Each of these offers something to quench your thirst; they will, I hope, also *increase* your thirst. Much like our physical body's need, our spiritual thirst is new every day and calls out for fresh quenching morning by morning.

I echo the poet of Psalm 42. I feel as though he had us in mind so many years ago when he wrote:

> As the deer pants for streams of water,
> so my soul pants for you, O God.
> My soul thirsts for God, for the living God.
> When can I go and meet with God? (1–2)

Part One:

COME TO THE WATER

THE SAMARITAN WOMAN'S STORY

John 4:4–19, 25–30, 39

Now he had to go through Samaria. So he came to a town in Samaria called Sychar, near the plot of ground Jacob had given to his son Joseph. Jacob's well was there, and Jesus, tired as he was from the journey, sat down by the well. It was about the sixth hour.

When a Samaritan woman came to draw water, Jesus said to her, "Will you give me a drink?" (His disciples had gone into the town to buy food.)

The Samaritan woman said to him, "You are a Jew and I am a Samaritan woman. How can you ask me for a drink?" (For Jews do not associate with Samaritans.)

Jesus answered her, "If you knew the gift of God and who it is that asks you for a drink, you would have asked him and he would have given you living water."

"Sir, the woman said, "you have nothing to draw with and the well is deep. Where can you get this living water? Are you greater than our father Jacob, who gave us the well and drank from it himself, as did also his sons and his flocks and his herds?"

Jesus answered, "Everyone who drinks this water will be thirsty again. But whoever drinks the water I give him will never thirst. Indeed, the water I give him will become in him a spring of water welling up to eternal life."

The woman said to him, "Sir, give me this water so that I don't get thirsty and have to keep coming here to draw water."

He told her, "Go call your husband and come back."

"I have no husband," she replied.

Jesus said to her, "You are right when you say you have no husband. The fact is, you have had five husbands, and the man you now have is not your husband. What you have just said is quite true."

"Sir," the woman said, "I can see that you are a prophet."

The woman said, "I know that the Messiah" (called Christ) "is coming. When he comes he will explain everything to us."

Then Jesus declared, "I who speak to you am he."

Just then his disciples returned and were surprised to find him talking with a woman. But no one asked, "What do you want?" or "Why are you talking with her?"

Then, leaving her water jar, the woman went back to town and said to the people, "Come, see a man who told me everything I ever did. Could this be the Christ?" They came out of the town and made their way toward him.

Many of the Samaritans from that town believed in him because of the woman's testimony, "He told me everything I ever did."

CHAPTER ONE

THE PATH LESS
TRAVELED

I rinsed out the fifty-gallon metal water tank with a hose
attached to the barn water hydrant. My horses nosed around
me, pushing at the tank and at me, asking for a drink. I reposi-
tioned the giant tank and stuck in the hose. Cool, clear well water
edged around the basin and the horses stuck their noses in, hap-
pily slurping and swallowing the fresh water. I patted their sun-
warmed necks and walked back to the barn, thinking about my
busy day ahead. My to-do list ticked in my head as I finished the
barn chores, went to the house, changed my clothes, and got in
my car to tend to all my errands.

Several hours later I came home. As soon as I walked in the
door of the house I knew there was a problem. From the basement I could hear the unmistakable wheezing and grinding of
the water pump. Immediately knowing I'd made a huge mistake,
I dashed to the barn, yanked down the water hydrant handle, and
looked out across the horses' pasture. They stood with curious
expressions in the middle of a miniature pond and nearly knee-

deep mud. It was as if they were thinking, *We didn't need* this *much water.*

Our private well is deep, with four-gallons-a-minute pressure. I didn't want to do the math: five hours times four gallons a *minute*?! In the house each time I tried the faucet the pipes coughed and spit gritty trickles with huge belches of air. The well was dry all right. Bone dry. Twenty-four-hours-before-it-would-be-replenished dry.

It was a bonehead mistake. A preventable mistake. A mistake I didn't soon forget as we thirsted for our well water over the next day.

It's also a mistake that parallels my spiritual life. I've been distracted and rushed on to the next thing on my list. Different demands called my name and I obligingly answered while ignoring the call in my spirit for refreshment. I ran on empty until my soul was sputtering, crying out for Living Water.

THE CROSSROADS OF NEED AND WILL

Have you found yourself in a similar desert of thirst? Thirst marks the crossroads of Need and Will. Physical thirst calls us to drink water—satisfying a need in our bodies designed by a Mighty Hand, which if unmet leads to death.

In a divine parallel, spiritual thirst also signposts the crossroads of our soul need and self-will. At the crossroads of Need and Will stands a choice. To which path will we set our feet? Maybe we'll follow the route lined with signs of many others passing before us. It's clearly marked, well worn, easy to follow. And isn't that a pool of water not too far distant?

Or will we start down the other path—the one that doesn't

look as well traveled? But there is something about it that's intriguing. A sense of promise seems to radiate from around the first corner. And is that the sound of a thundering waterfall in the distance?

Your mouth is starting to feel a little dry looking at the pool down one path and hearing the cascade down the other. So which path will you choose?

The first will only temporarily seem better—because the pool of water isn't fresh. It's really a mired water hole from which everyone drinks. Polluted and overused, it has no sustaining value.

But the second path ... The echoing distant waterfall is indeed as complete and fulfilling and everlasting as the promise you sense at the crossroads. Because it is fed by the river of Living Water.

The future-fulfilled promise beckoning to you from the hidden cascade is the righteous life. A life that lives on the water of who Christ is. A life that is daily sustained by the refreshment of the Holy Spirit. A life that doesn't run dry when demands threaten to suck every last drop from your soul. Why? Because at the waterfall fed by the river of Living Water, you will arrive at God's dwelling place, where you will live next to, be sustained by, and feel fully satisfied through the Living Water of Christ.

THIRSTING FOR RIGHTEOUSNESS

We thirst for many things: recognition, prosperity, family, a great job. But they are only temporary thirst-quenchers, aren't they? Because we learn with each acquisition that our spiritual tanks spring even more leaks of dissatisfaction, leading us to thirst again.

What we are truly thirsting for is something that will keep our spiritual reserves topped off. "Things" aren't going to do it. A better job or a bigger house or better relationships aren't going to meet the thirst. They only wet our whistle. We need something to *quench* our thirst.

> WHAT WE ARE THIRSTING FOR IS A DEEP, ABIDING, NEVER-RUN-DRY, LOVE-RELATIONSHIP WITH GOD.

What we are thirsting for is a deep, abiding, never-run-dry, love-relationship with God. Psalm 119:152 reads, "Long ago I learned from your statutes that you established them to last forever." The intent of God's Word, and therefore our relationship with Him, is designed to be eternal. Why is a love-relationship with the Lord and His Word our thirst-quencher? Because He is the only one who has the sustaining properties our souls need to stay hydrated. What are they? Unconditional love, forgiveness, faithfulness, eternal life, acceptance, peace, and a heavenly inheritance (to name just a few). Sound mouth-watering, don't they? We may already know these are God's traits, so why do we still feel thirsty? Because we are thirsting to *live on* those qualities of God. We need to ingest them, ruminate on them, and let them sustain us. We are thirsting for a life that reflects a cup overflowing with His righteousness in us.

Matthew 5:6 promises, "Blessed are those who hunger and thirst for righteousness, for they will be filled." We thirst for a righteous life because we know separate from the righteousness found in Christ we have no life.

The verse says we are blessed *because* we thirst. The blessing comes not only in the filling but also in the thirsting. The words "will be" speak of the future. We "will be" filled, but along the way there "will be" a process. Part of that process is the thirst sensation. We have to take those initial tottering steps of faith down the more inviting but less traveled path, confident of the promise of Christ's Living Water.

BROKEN PROMISES

God keeps His promises. That is part of His very essence. He doesn't make promises He can't, won't, or has no intention of keeping. We, on the other hand, make promises of a different sort—we bend and break them to suit our convenience.

We all know the pain of broken promises. In the wake of an unkept promise flows the full range of human emotions: disappointment, shattered hearts, dashed dreams, lost hope.

No one knew more about the pain of broken promises than the Samaritan woman at the well. I wish she'd been given a name. Yet her anonymity feels familiar to us. She was labeled as "that sinful woman" and rejected by her community. Her lack of personal identification is a result of broken promises. Brokenness was a lifestyle to her: a broken heart, broken marriages, broken dreams. She was even broken and separate from her community and other women. Walking alone to the well every day, carrying her empty water vessels, only served to remind her of her empty life. The more brokenness dictated her life, the more she felt certain that wholeness was someone else's inheritance.

We can identify with the broken promises of her life. We feel hurt, unfulfilled, and burdened with unkept promises—some by our own doing and others at the hands of careless people.

As in any marriage, my husband, Peter, and I have experienced valleys of disappointment and mountains of hurt. We've angered each other and disappointed one another. Nearly twenty years ago we made our marriage vows to one another to "love, honor, and cherish" until death separated us. Though honest and heartfelt, we've still hurt each other.

During one particular valley of discouragement we decided to go kayaking with our children at our favorite pond. We paddled across the pond to a giant boulder, and while the children paddled and swam, Peter and I climbed up the sun-warmed rock. We both sighed, a shared heaviness between us. Finally I broke our muteness and said, "Where can we go to start over?" I didn't mean a physical, geographical place; I meant a place inside each of us where we could turn our backs on the mutual hurt and choose to forgive and try again. We talked for a long time, and finally, sore from sitting so long on the rock, we paddled back across the pond. But we had arrived at a new starting place. And that giant boulder became the altar where we left behind our hurts and disappointments.

Remember that when we experience hurt and disappointment and brokenness, it's always the result of our own unmet expectations of ourselves or other people. All disappointment is people-generated. We need to take and accept ownership of it. Even though God has always been at the heart of our marriage, it wasn't His fault that Peter and I had hurt each other.

WE NEED TO LOOK TO OUR HEALER AND KEEPER OF PROMISES TO FILL OUR THIRST FOR WHOLENESS.

The two of us now understand that in the wake of brokenness and pain is a thirst for something better. We have a desire not only for healing but also for a new place in our souls where we can start over. We need to look to our Healer and Keeper of Promises to fill our thirst for wholeness.

FULFILLED PROMISES

The story of the Samaritan woman takes place in a town called Sychar, where Jacob's well had provided water to the townspeople for many years (John 4:5). It stood as a tribute not only to Jacob (later renamed Israel) and his descendants, but even more it symbolized God's faithfulness to the nation of Israel. In all those years it hadn't run dry. The well was deep and abiding—just like the Lord himself.

To the Samaritan woman it took on an even more personal symbol. Because the well had always been there in her lifetime, it felt like a place of refuge for her. It had never proved unfaithful to her. The one thing she could count on in her broken life was the ready and true supply of water from Jacob's well.

Then Jesus came. Since the well is where she daily walked to fill her physical thirst, this would be the logical place for Christ to meet her to fill her spiritual thirst.

The well was the only secure thing in her life. She *expected* to come away with her thirst quenched and her water jars filled. On that day she couldn't have known she would come away with a greater thirst also satisfied.

Christ's meeting the Samaritan woman at Jacob's well was also the fulfillment of God's promise. Jesus Christ was the promised Redeemer in the flesh. The nation of Israel had been promised through prophecy that from Jacob's offspring and through the house of David a Redeemer would be born to the world. This inherited promise was anticipated from generation to generation until it came to fruition through a virgin's womb (see Matthew, chapter 1). The full circle of God's promised Redeemer was shrink-wrapped and time-warped into this preordained meeting between the woman and Christ. Thirst no more, wait no longer—the Redeemer had arrived to fill the spiritual longing that not only she yearned for but that we also do.

Remarkably, the revelation of this promise was exposed through a sinner! Jesus used sinners along His path to teach those around Him. Because we all "fall short of the glory of God" (Romans 3:23), what better way to point out our shortcomings than by illustrating our commonality through others?

All her adult life the Samaritan woman had searched for something that man could not fill. We too thirst for something that the pleasures of man cannot quench. Just as the woman learned, there isn't some *thing* that will satisfy our longing for fulfillment. There is only *Some One* who will.

Jesus Christ is the fulfillment of the promise of Jacob's well. He is the fulfillment of the promised Redeemer. He is the fulfillment of the promise of restoration. All the brokenness and emptiness that we shoulder each day is restored to wholeness and refilled with Christ's Living Water. He said, "Whoever drinks the water I give him will never thirst. Indeed, the water I give him will become in him a spring of water welling up to eternal life" (John 4:14).

FOLLOWING THE ROAD LESS TRAVELED

A promise was fulfilled for us too that day at Jacob's well. It's the promise of eternal life available through our Redeemer.

By His grace we hold promise too. We are redeemable. We are worth His time and words and life. Of course He wants to see us free from burdens and full of promise. That's the point of His free gift of salvation—He's the Redeemer of the redeemable.

At the outset of this journey to the thirst-quenching blessing of the righteous life, we need to leave our burdens at the crossroads of Need and Will. Our burdens of hurt, expectations we have of

> BY HIS GRACE WE HOLD
> PROMISE TOO. WE ARE
> REDEEMABLE.

others and of ourselves, and broken promises—all are luggage we can't carry with us. We need to take this journey empty-handed, ready to receive what the Lord has in store for us along the way.

The Samaritan woman took the well-traveled road to Jacob's well. It was a familiar dusty, worn path. But she returned by a new route. The one less traveled, edged with redemption and promise. Will you follow in her footsteps?

Draw Near to Him:

God's promises for us are daily and eternal. Think about and ask the Lord to call to mind what promises in your life He has fulfilled. Write these in your journal as a reminder of His faithfulness.

Drink From His Cup:

"Christ redeemed us from the curse of the law by becoming a curse for us, for it is written, 'Cursed is everyone who is hung on a tree.' He redeemed us in order that the blessing given to Abraham might come to the Gentiles through Christ Jesus, so that by faith we might receive the promise of the Spirit" (Galatians 3:13–14).

CHAPTER TWO

DRAWING NEAR

I am drawn to the sound of water. Maybe I feel the pull of water because my maiden name is Marriner and my sailing heritage desires to answer the call of open water. From the lap of waves on the hull of my kayak, to the springtime gushing stream in the valley of our property, to the crashing waves of the New Hampshire coast, the sights and sounds fill me with feelings of well-being.

I can step out of my house in the spring and stand on the deck listening for the overflowing stream, breathe deep, and feel as if the sound of the life-giving water renews my internal life. It's authentic and restorative and pure.

It's a sound and feeling that can't be replicated, though. Knowing how much I love the sound of streams, my husband bought me a miniature fountain for our home. I gathered a few stones, filled the small reservoir with water, plugged it in, and heard an instant trickling stream. This just didn't cut it. My mind could not be tricked into believing this was a real, outdoor stream. There's a depth of sound, a timbre—or quality—that cannot be reproduced in a manufactured box.

It's this same depth of sound and quality of the flowing water that we desire to fill our parched souls. The purity of Christ's Living Water can't be reproduced by anything else. Buying more, owning bigger, and living expansively empties more than our wallets. Our souls are spent too. The "things" we gather in our lives, hoping they will satisfy our yearnings, only end up feeling empty and stale. We need the depth and timbre and quality and clarity only found in the real thing.

Christ's Living Water is an external source to meet an internal need with the benefit of eternal life. This journey to the source of God's Living Water will quench our thirst for Him and His Lordship in our lives.

> CHRIST'S LIVING WATER IS AN EXTERNAL SOURCE TO MEET AN INTERNAL NEED WITH THE BENEFIT OF ETERNAL LIFE.

Just as I can't ignore the gentle sounds of water drawing me closer to its source, neither could the Samaritan woman ignore the tantalizing words Christ spoke about Eternal Water. He asked her to draw nearer, step by hesitant step, as He talked to her about *her* life. She found herself lost to what she knew and drawn to what she did not know.

Christ's words felt fresh to her, new and sparkling like a pure flowing stream. His words wooed her, drew her closer, and asked her to take steps she wouldn't have dared to take before. How did He do that? He talked to her in a familiar way that proved He *knew* her—inside and out.

HE KNOWS THE EXTERNAL

I have no doubt Jesus knew the Samaritan woman's name. So why didn't He use it? He relayed to her the sordid truths of her personal life. Again, why? Because He knew these were the ways the community defined her and she defined herself: labeled by her illicit lifestyle, but not worthy of a name. Jesus wanted her to know the externals of her life weren't as important as who she was *to Him*. Her labels didn't matter to Him.

We wear labels too. Like Hawthorne's *Scarlet Letter*, we wear our own red marks of sin and bad choices and hard lives. The marks of who we are may be as distinct as the rumpled clothes we don each day or the extra worry lines across our foreheads.

If you've ever spent time with a person with low self-esteem, you know firsthand the self-conscious, self-deprecating remarks a person can say about herself. "I'm such a loser." "Well, that was dumb." "I'll never get anywhere." These easily become self-fulfilling prophesies. If what you say about yourself is the best you believe of yourself, that's the best you will become.

Jesus sees and knows these external marks and labels. But He doesn't call us by the same definition we have of ourselves. He doesn't call us "the low self-esteemed one" or "the prideful one" or "the wealthy one" or "the well-dressed one" or "the black-haired, brown-eyed one."

When we are called to the side of Jacob's well, we are called by the names He knows us as: "loved one" (1 John 4:9–11), "treasure" (Deuteronomy 7:6), and "friend" (John 15:13–15). We respond with confidence to the call of these new names because all our self-expectations and those of others are no longer valid. We are the wearers of new labels.

It reminds me of when my son began to pull himself up on the furniture, trying to imitate the rest of the walking world around him. He was a half-crawler and had learned how to sit and scoot and roll to where he wanted to be. He was nine months old when one day all his coordination clicked in, and he pulled himself up on a chair and simply walked right across the room. No falling, no tipping over, no sitting hard on his rump. He left the label of "scooter" behind and instantly became a "walker."

Our Redeemer christens us with a new label too. We are forever after known as "The Redeemed One." We belong to Christ and we wear the banner of "Christian" as proof of our new label. "Therefore, if anyone is in Christ, he is a new creation; the old has gone, the new has come" (2 Corinthians 5:17).

HE KNOWS THE INTERNAL

When Jesus didn't speak the Samaritan woman's name, He showed He was more interested in what was inside her than what was going on outside. As is always the case with our Lord, He touches the inside to transform the outside.

> OUR LORD TOUCHES THE INSIDE TO TRANSFORM THE OUTSIDE.

Jesus always wants to reach deeper into our beings than merely touch what's visible to the world. The invisible is where the changes in our lives take place, where He touches our deepest place of need, our hurts, our hopes, and our secrets.

Christ meets us with full knowledge of who we are. We aren't a mystery to Him. He knows what motivates us, the sins of our lives, and the hopes of our hearts. Yet we only know a part of Him. It takes us more than a lifetime to have full understanding of Him, because we won't know all the mysteries of God this side of heaven.

It's as if we have a small balance scale in our hearts. On one side is the weight of sin. On the other is Christ. When we come into knowledge of Him as Savior, the scale tips in His favor because He takes away our sins. As only we can so blithely do, though, sin tiptoes back onto the scale and begins to weigh us down again. What we need to do is replace the sin side with Christ's character. Something has to fill the void where we've removed sin or hurt. Christ wants to refill it with a revelation of who He is.

We need Christ on both sides of the scales of our hearts so no sin will rule over us or overweight our balance. An exchange needs to take place. When we are honest with ourselves and allow the Holy Spirit to reveal pieces of ourselves that need transforming, that piece is then removed from the scale and replaced by a piece of Christlikeness.

What is meant by being "honest with ourselves" about sin? Psalm 19:12–13 reminds us, "Who can discern his errors? Forgive my hidden faults. Keep your servant also from willful sins; may they not rule over me." Willful sins are those we commit knowing they are sin, yet do them anyway because we either know we can ask forgiveness (cheap grace) or we are being defiant. Willful sins can be as small as gossip or rudeness and as large as murder.

When the scales of our hearts are balanced, we no longer live by our will; therefore willful sins cannot have lordship over us. Psalm 119:133–134 says, "Direct my footsteps according to your word; let no sin rule over me. Redeem me from the oppression of men, that I may obey your precepts." Walking in God's Word and being obedient to it assures us of not overbalancing the scales with our own human willfulness.

The Lord understands this inner battle between our will and His Word. All sins originate from willfulness. But willfulness dissipates when we listen to His Word. First John 3:20 assures us:

"For God is greater than our hearts, and he knows everything." The choice is ours: to listen to our inner willful self, or to listen to Him.

HE KNOWS THE ETERNAL

The Lord sees our external person, He's familiar with our internal person, but He is most concerned with our *eternal* person.

The Lord is always for us. If our souls didn't matter to Him, He wouldn't have found them worthy to die for. But obviously we matter very much to Him.

We lose sight of the fact that we are here on earth for a very short time. God's true intent, His real desire, is for us to be at home in heaven with Him. He calls us His family, and like any parent He wants His family near Him.

Because God knows eternity from the beginning until now and beyond, we have mere years for our souls to be impacted by what Christ did. The New Testament communicates a sense of urgency about preaching and teaching the gospel and winning souls for the Lord.

The Samaritan woman was baptized with a sense of urgency as soon as Jesus revealed himself to her. The woman made a headlong flight back to town because the Lord had known who she was, loved her anyway, and told her how she'd live forever on His Living Water. Talk about instant transformation! She went from a silent, sullen, guilt-ridden woman to an outspoken witness.

Two wrongs make a right when imperfect people with imperfect skills perform God's perfect will. That's the Samaritan woman all right. She'd had a wrong life, she hadn't developed the right evangelistic skills yet, but she performed God's perfect will: that of bringing the souls of others to the Lord.

That's what the eternal Jesus is after. He's not only our personal soul-winner but also the winner of the souls of whole communities.

GOING THE DISTANCE

I like to take a walk each day, but if I'm by myself I can't seem to walk more than a mile and a half. I get bored with the sound of my own footfalls. Insipid songs repeat themselves in my brain, and I feel impatient to get home to do something else. But when I walk with my children or my husband or friends, I can walk for miles upon miles. We never seem to run out of things to say or creation to look at. Five miles pass under our feet in a flash.

The worn road to Jacob's well was well traveled and known. Conversations and chatter filled the air back and forth to the well. How lonely it must have been, then, for the Samaritan woman to walk the path by herself, left to thinking her own thoughts.

Yet walking alone on that hot day is what gave her the opportunity to speak alone with Jesus. She went the full distance to the well, even though it felt like the least comfortable thing to do. Similar to how I feel on my solitary walks, maybe she arrived at her destination impatient just to fill her jar and trudge back home.

She wouldn't have gotten her water if she didn't go the whole way to the well. This concept may seem overly simplistic, but consider this: We too easily get discouraged by the journey required to reach the well, and we sometimes give up before getting there. Yes, it is a solitary walk sometimes. Yes, it can feel endless and uncomfortable. But as the woman learned through the time of quiet reflection with Christ, she became ready to receive what He had to give her.

GOING DIFFERENT DISTANCES

When Peter and I met we were joggers. We'd run up to five miles a day—together or separately. Shortly before we were married we decided to train for a 6K race. We both put a lot of effort into preparing for the race, and when the day arrived it was a pleasant seventy-degree, overcast day. Good running weather. The other racers weren't just joggers like Peter and me, simply out for a pleasant run, they were *runners*—people who used measly 6K races as training for the big ones—the 10Ks and the marathons.

Peter and I ran the race, our strides matched throughout, and finished at respectable times. But we never jogged again. It wasn't because we didn't need the exercise anymore; it wasn't even that the race was that difficult. I believe we never ran again because we weren't *runners*. We didn't have the heart or the drive to do it again or a desire to progress to bigger races. Six kilometers was our distance.

HE IS A GRACIOUS GOD; HE WANTS TO SEE US SUCCEED.

But the other runners, the ones passing us at breakneck speeds with eyes glued to the horizon, could go a different distance than us. Their bodies were more prepared and they had minds trained for the endurance required in longer races.

It's the same in our faith journeys. We all go different

distances. The distance I go to reach the well is different than the distance you will be required to go. Since the Lord has designed us as individuals, our walks with Him will also be individually tailored to what He plans for us. Some of us are endurance runners in our faith journeys. We are the ones who are tested over and over and over and found faithfully prepared. Others of us are short-distance runners. Because the Lord knows if we're tested too much we'll stumble and fall. He is a gracious God; He wants to see us succeed.

MISDIRECTION

We have to go the full distance to the well where Jesus beckons us. Sometimes the problem is that we *think* we're preparing for the distance, we *think* we're on the right track, we *think* we're doing the right things to arrive safely. My question is, *why don't we KNOW?*

There is a difference between motion and direction. We sometimes go through the motions in our faith journeys. We get involved in lots of "Christian" activities in the name of serving the Lord. However, they are truly just activities if you personally have not been called to them. Though they may be worthwhile and noble causes, if God hasn't called you to them, you are walking down the wrong path to the wrong well.

Conversely, *direction* is when you *know* you are on the right path. You know you've been called to the various positions of ministry or work. God's plan for your life is as clear to you as the water that is drawn from His well.

Easy for me to say; harder to live by? It seems so many people feel uncertain about God's call for them. This may not be the answer you want to hear, but if you're having a hard time hearing

God's call, it probably isn't because He's not speaking loud enough.

Sometimes we have misdirected steps because we haven't waited for a confirmation of the Lord's calling. Sometimes we are impatient to get "into" the call, so we jump ahead, knowing what the call is but over-anticipating the timing. Sometimes we create our own plan because it seems the Lord doesn't have one for us, or worse, we don't like what He has for us.

These are poor excuses for bad listening skills. The only way we are going to correctly hear God's call for direction is to spend quality time with Him.

God is looking for trustworthy partners. People who will share in and obediently carry His vision for the world's souls.

John 21:15–19 communicates one of the last verbal directions Jesus gave to His disciples. He confronted Peter and asked him to take care of the flocks of people who needed to know about the Risen Savior. Then Jesus stood up and walked away from the morning fire by the Sea of Tiberias, where they had been eating breakfast. He turned to Peter and said, "Follow me." What did He mean? In essence, "This is the direction you are now to walk in. Not following your own way, not following other people, not following tradition. But following *me*. Follow in my footsteps, follow my path, and follow my voice."

We can be certain of God's direct call on our lives when we are tuned to His voice. The way to be tuned to His voice is to expect to hear it. Just as I recognize my children's voices in a room filled with other children's voices and noises, we too need to recognize God's voice in all situations.

Starting in the quiet places of our lives equips us to then be able to hear Him in the busy places. Spending time in His Word, reading books about Him and His character, listening to good, scriptural, godly teaching, and having quality prayer time all serve to open our ears.

> TIME SPENT WITH GOD
> IS NOT TIME SPENT,
> IT'S TIME INVESTED.

Time spent with God is not time *spent,* it's time *invested.* It's time invested because through prayer He will lead you in the direction He wants you to go. Time in prayer is never merely for current needs, it's for future seeking. You are investing in your future when you spend time with God.

FEELINGS WON'T MAKE THE DISTANCE

If we depend solely on our *feelings* during our faith journeys, we won't make the distance. We'll get discouraged, we'll want to give up, we'll feel complacent, we'll feel spiritually fatigued. These all drain our commitment reservoirs.

In the movie *As Good As It Gets,* actor Jack Nicholson portrays a psychologically challenged individual. At one point he is leaving his psychiatrist's office and he stops in the middle of the waiting room and says to the other patients, "What if this is as good as it gets?"

That's a question I have asked myself. There's fear in that statement. There's complacency too. What if it never gets any better than this, and am I willing to live this way for the rest of my life?

We find ourselves stuck in this place when we are in the pit of discouragement. Indeed, what if this _____ (fill in the blank—house, relationship, job, child, etc.) is the best God has for me? Am I willing to live out my life like this?

But when we are "in Christ" it's not our life to live. Being "in Christ" means we've died to our own ambitions for our lives. We don't have ownership, He does.

> BUT WHEN WE ARE
>
> "IN CHRIST"
>
> IT'S NOT OUR LIFE TO LIVE.

When my son, now twelve, was diagnosed at six with insulin-injection-dependent diabetes, one of my first questions was, "Lord, this is the *best* you have for Jordan? How can this devastating disease be your *best* for this child and our family?" I learned the revelation that God's sovereignty will be magnified in any situation if we look for and allow His glory to reign.

SEEING HIS GLORY

Maybe you're shaking your head and thinking, "But I was abused" or "My husband left me for another woman" or "I'm a young widow" or "My only child is dead." Painful? Most certainly and beyond compare. Insurmountable? No.

Was God looking the other way when these horrible things happened? There is an unshakable truth about the Lord. God never looks the other way. You have never been out of His sight or out of His reach or away from His heart. Though you may not understand the circumstances or have the answers you want to hear this side of heaven, God does have the answers and He does know the reasons and He was *right by your side* through every lonely and confusing step.

When Lazarus, beloved brother of Mary and Martha, died, what was Christ's response? "Did I not tell you that if you believed, you would see the glory of God?" (See John 11.) Does this mean that to be able to see the glory of God we have to believe His glory can come from a bad or hurtful or sad situation? Yes. Recognizing His glory, even in places and situations that we are unhappy or hurt about, transforms our view of it being a "bad" thing.

NO MORE DEFEAT

> JESUS TRANSFORMS EVERYTHING: US, AND OUR SITUATIONS.

Jesus transforms everything: us, and our situations. Only a divine, loving, and all-powerful God could transform what is devastating to something good.

We need to equip ourselves with the basic requirements of courage, strength, and stamina to be able to see and testify to God's glory. If we live defeated by awful situations, then we aren't claiming the victory of the Cross. Jesus defeated our defeat. He was and is victorious. When He hung on the cross and breathed His last words, "It is finished," He meant defeatism was finished. *He* wasn't finished; His work wasn't finished. But defeat was finished.

Hebrews 12:2–3 reminds us, "Let us fix our eyes on Jesus, the author and perfecter of our faith, who for the joy set before him endured the cross, scorning its shame, and sat down at the right hand of the throne of God. Consider him who endured such opposition from sinful men, so that you will not grow weary and lose heart." When our eyes are "fixed" on Christ and not our circumstances, our faith journeys can be perfected. When our hearts are "fixed" on Christ we have courage stored up in our souls to keep walking toward the well.

THE CHOICE IS ALWAYS YOURS

One of the greatest truths of Christianity is that it's based on free choice. Down the annals of time, from Adam and Eve's bite into the fruit to you and me bearing their sin-mark, we each have been given the gift of choice from God.

It's the choice of eternal life. We could reject it. We could turn our backs on the Lord's voice. But like the Samaritan woman, let's come close to the edge of the well and look into Christ's eyes as He confronts and comforts us. His helping hand is extended to us if we just step a little closer as a sign of agreement to choose to walk in a deep love-relationship on this journey with Him.

Draw Near to Him:

What distance are you willing to go to the well? Will you go the whole way, listening to His encouraging voice? How can you claim Christ's victory over painful areas of defeat in your life?

Drink From His Cup:

"Blessed are those whose strength is in you, who have set their hearts on pilgrimage" (Psalm 84:5).

CHAPTER THREE

NO TURNING BACK

G od isn't into reruns. He doesn't have a giant VCR in heaven to watch instant replays of us messing up. The *consequences* of our mistakes may shadow our steps, but God doesn't want us to relive poor choices over and over.

We are the ones who replay our internal videos. We are a patterned people—patterned in our thoughts and actions. Unhealthy patterns are habitual holes into which we keep falling.

GULLY WASHES

Our farm property is a natural watershed—two hills sloping down into a valley. On one side of the valley is our house, barn, and small horse pastures. On the other side are fenced fields and woods. Dividing the watershed is a brook that runs into a swamp. Over the years of winter snow runoff and heavy spring rains the brook has dug its way through and around dirt and rocks, forming a riverbed of up to three to four feet deep. The watercourse has smoothed rocks and eaten away at solid ground, leaving a distinct gully, even if barely a trickle runs through it in the heat of summer.

Like a gully wash for storm water runoff, the patterns of our lives keep returning us to the lowest points. The more often we return to these gullies, the more erosion takes place. Little pieces of our self-esteem, values, and beliefs get carried downstream and can't be reclaimed.

Some of us have Grand Canyon–sized gullies in our lives. The height of the walls around us feels insurmountable as we are continuously carried along in the same deep patterns we have always followed. But when Jesus touches our heart and conscience we are redirected to a new route. He lifts us out of the gully washes. We don't need to keep following the lowest points of the riverbeds and rerunning the same gullies. He doesn't want to see us return to the same places in our hearts and minds, because they are unsafe pits.

Yet what is it about the gullies that keeps attracting our attention? Above the gullies we are exposed and at risk of discovery. But the eroded depths feel safe and secret because they are familiar. We continue to get swept along because we think these places will satisfy our recurrent thirst. We are remedial learners at best. We keep trying to satisfy the thirst with the same things that have never worked before. And each time the erosion gets worse.

Returning to familiar ways is reminiscent of Lot's wife, isn't it? Her hometown of Sodom was destined for destruction because of blatant immorality. Two angels visited Lot and his family, warned them of impending

SALT PROVOKES THIRST, AND THE PILLAR OF SALT SERVES TO REMIND US OF A THIRST UNMET IN SODOM.

disaster, and then escorted them out of the doomed city. The angels' parting words to Lot and his family were to run and not look back. "But Lot's wife looked back, and she became a pillar of salt" (Genesis 19:26). Why did she look back? Curiosity? Defiance? Disbelief? Longing? Sadness? Each one of these reasons may be why she made that fatal about-face, but fast-forward to the twenty-first century, and those same reasons are why we continuously turn our eyes to idols. Even more interesting is the answer to why she was turned into a pillar of salt. Why not a stone, or why not just strike her dead? Salt provokes thirst, and the pillar of salt serves to remind us of a thirst unmet in Sodom. What things did Lot's wife look back at that had failed to meet her thirst in Sodom? *Idols.*

IDOLATRY

Idolatry temporarily gratifies a need—the need to feel fulfilled or satisfied. We feel lonely and empty; we eat to fill a void. Food becomes an idol. An unhealthy weight results. Or we spend an inordinate amount of time staying in shape. Our bodies become an idol. Or we feel a need to escape reality, so we spend hours watching television. Personal escape and avoidance are idols.

Idolatry is also defined as something that holds control over us. Compulsive gambling, eating disorders, viewing pornography, and using drugs or alcohol all have their roots in self-gratification. The addictive behavior controls the person. Because our heavenly Father wants to be in control of every part of our being, anything that isn't under His control is idolatry.

Some of us have been taught that only tangible items or material possessions are idols, or "golden calves," as the Old Testament notes. That's not entirely true. Idols can be anything that holds a "golden" place in our hearts. Attitudes can be idols. Actions can be idols. Our work can be our idol.

Any idol is externally measurable by our senses. And it easily happens. After all, we can see our figures in the mirror; we can't see God. We think we can see the profit from being a workaholic, but we don't always readily see God's hand at work. It's much easier to base our feelings of satisfaction on what our five senses tell us.

Mature Christians learn to base their feelings of fulfillment on their soul's voice. Worshiping the Lord wholeheartedly has an internally measurable result. "Renewed in knowledge in the image of its Creator" (Colossians 3:10) means not using idols to try to satisfy a need. Instead, our minds need to be filled with the knowledge of God. We need to leave behind what we know, what we think will satisfy our thirst. We have to decide to take a new route rather than returning to the same old gullies.

> WORSHIPING THE LORD WHOLEHEARTEDLY HAS AN INTERNALLY MEASURABLE RESULT.

NO TWO WAYS ABOUT IT

It's easy for us to say of Lot's wife, "*Tsk, tsk,* she shouldn't have looked baaack." But don't we too keep looking over our shoulders or worse, try to straddle the familiar gullies of idolatry? We figure we're not stepping fully into the pit, we're just "seeing what it's all about." The Bible says that double-mindedness promotes instability (James 1:8). Like Lot's wife, it's not even safe for us to walk near the gullies. We'd just keep falling in. God tells us not to walk near them and not to look back. We can't have it both ways.

First Kings challenges us about double-mindedness: "How long will you waver between two opinions? If the Lord is God, follow him; but if Baal is God, follow him" (18:21). It's a one-way street. It's been said you can't have "just enough Jesus to keep you out of hell."

Our encounters with Christ force us to make a decision: Keep the familiar idols in our hearts, or trust in the Lord to satisfy our thirst. Divine and new understanding is ours when we *know* He will satisfy all the needs we have in our lives that we have unsuccessfully tried to fill with the pleasures of this life.

Psalm 90:14 assures us that at the dawn of a new day of understanding He will satisfy us. "Satisfy us in the morning with your unfailing love, that we may sing for joy and be glad all our days." His abiding *love* is what will satisfy all those things that idols never can or did. And what follows? Unceasing joy and gladness, because they come from our internal relationship *with God*—not an external replacement *for Him*.

ARRIVING WITH EXPECTANCY

The stream that divides our farm in half starts far back in our woodlands, where the watershed is steeper and giant boulders cling to the hillsides. Shortly after purchasing our property Peter and I followed the stream deep into the woods and came to a place where a steep hill plateaued above the riverbed. I said to him, "This is where I want my cabin." Fifteen years later he built me a cabin on that very spot.

A couple of years ago, in late October, just as the trees scratched their stripped branches across the gray skies overhead, Peter used his tractor and a chainsaw to cut a wood's road part of the way to the building site. But from the end of the narrow trail up to the clearing, all the needed building materials were carried on his, a friend's, or my shoulders. Using a measuring tape, chainsaw, hammer, and nails he built "High Places" (see Habakkuk 3:18–19 AMP), my cabin, with three windows, a sleeping loft, a woodstove, a futon couch, and a writing table.

Trudging up the well-worn path through the fall leaves and early snows, we came to understand the value of economy and efficiency. Our motto became "Don't come up empty-handed." There was always *something* that needed to be carried from the end of the wood's road to the cabin.

> WHEN WE ARRIVE WITH EXPECTATION, WE ARE COMING TO THE LORD EMPTY OF OURSELVES.

The Lord took those very words we spoke and entrusted me with a deeper understanding: Don't arrive at His well empty-handed. Arrive with a receptacle that can be filled with His Living Water. We need to arrive at His side with expectancy.

We need to *plan on* being filled when we arrive at the well. How silly to go to the well of Living Water and not have a container to use for gathering and holding the Water! Yet that's exactly what we do. We arrive with all sorts of excuses as to why we don't have any gathering equipment. "I'm too tired" or "I lost my water container." But those excuses are centered in self-pity.

When we arrive with expectation, we are coming to the Lord empty of ourselves. *We* are the empty containers He needs to fill. When we arrive, our expectations aren't self-seeking or for self-gratification (do I hear the squeak of idolatry again?) but rather righteous anticipation of being filled with Him.

The prophet Haggai saw with clear eyes the connection between idolatry, thirst, selfish expectations, and God's fulfillment. Listen to the story:

> Now this is what the Lord Almighty says: "Give careful thought to your ways. You have planted much, but have harvested little. You eat, but never have enough. You drink, but never have your fill. You put on clothes, but are not warm. You earn wages, only to put them in a purse with holes in it."
>
> This is what the Lord Almighty says: "Give careful thought to your ways. Go up into the mountains and bring down timber and build the house, so that I may take pleasure in it and be honored," says the Lord. "You expected much, but see, it turned out to be little. What you brought home, I blew away. Why?" declares the Lord Almighty. "Because of my house which remains a ruin, while each of you is busy with his own house. Therefore, because of you the heavens have withheld their dew and the earth its crops. I called for a drought on the fields and the mountains, on the grain, the new wine, the oil and whatever the ground produces, on men and cattle, and on the labor of your hands" (Haggai 1:5–11).

Just a tad convicting! The people of Haggai's time had been busy building their own houses, fulfilling their own desires, and in the process ignoring God's house. They *expected* to find fulfillment and satisfaction in these things—"You expected much, but see, it turned out to be little." In their self-expectation the land experienced a drought, everything thirsted—the people, the land, and the livestock alike. Why? Because, like us, they worked for other things to fill their thirst.

But what are God's veiled words about the righteous lifestyle choice the people could make? Tend to Him, concentrate on His dwelling place, and then the thirsting would cease. In today's language the dwelling place that needs tending to is our inner being. Our soul is where Christ and the Holy Spirit live.

And what was required of the people? Hard work. "Go up into the mountains and bring down timber and build the house." In other words, don't use what you've got lying around here to build; your leftovers are useless for His purposes. But *go* and find fresh, straight, virgin forest to use.

They went all right. "The whole remnant of the people obeyed the voice of the Lord their God and the message of the prophet Haggai, because the Lord their God had sent him. And the people feared the Lord" (1:12). I'll bet the people didn't go up into those mountains empty-handed either. They went with axes and saws to cut the fresh wood for God's temple. They left behind those things that had not brought them fulfillment but had only brought drought. They went with eager expectation, armed for the task. They walked back down those mountains full of expectant joy, anticipating the Lord's glory.

> THEY LEFT BEHIND THOSE THINGS THAT HAD NOT BROUGHT THEM FULFILLMENT BUT HAD ONLY BROUGHT DROUGHT.

Then God spoke through Haggai: " 'The glory of this present house will be greater than the glory of the former house,' says the Lord Almighty. 'And in this place I will grant peace' " (2:9).

GOD'S FAVOR OF PEACE

The granting of peace is not a small offering from God. Haggai's people were a torn group. Historically and traditionally they were torn by war and disagreements. Personally they were worn out by the lack of fulfillment in their lives. Spiritually they were fragmented by confusion. The favor of peace was the greatest promise God could give them.

It's not so different than us. Our "former house," with idols decorating the walls of our hearts, is not a place of peace. Too many "things" are vying for attention. But in our new, "present" house, peace can be the framework of the entire structure. It is strong, secure, and built to withstand storms. Psalm 37:37 promises, "There is a future for the man of peace." In other words, when we have internal unshakable peace, it is transferred to external action. And therein is our future—a future of continued peace, a future of God's blessings and favor.

Psalm 119:165 says, "Great peace have they who love your law, and nothing can make them stumble." Not just a little bit of peace, but overflowing peace if we listen to and respect and obey God's Word. Then what does it say? "Nothing can make them stumble." This means as we take the new route, guided by God's Word, with peace as our companion, nothing will be able to reclaim our attention. Note it doesn't say we won't have any more obstacles along the way; it only says the obstacles won't make us stumble. In other words, we'll be given the strength and knowledge to get around them.

It's good to anticipate what those potential obstacles might be. They are the stones of hardship that Satan will roll into our paths. We have a choice to keep our peace or look at the stones. The stones that rob our peace can be little pebbles of irritation throughout our days—from backed-up traffic, to interruptions, to squabbling children. Or the stones can be as huge as boulders in the form of disappointment, grief, bitterness, or unforgiveness. Satan will use whatever we have a difficult time dealing with. Remember, Satan *lives* to see our peace *stolen*. It is one of his greatest tactics: to rob us of our peace and watch us stumble.

Colossians reminds us where our peace must dwell: "Let the peace of Christ rule in your hearts, since as members of one body you were called to peace" (Colossians 3:15). Peace should "rule in our hearts." Rule? Rule, govern, dictate, stand watch over, control. Peace ruling in our hearts will control all our thoughts and actions. When peace rules, the pebbles and stones won't irritate us or get in our way.

THE WELLSPRING OF HOPE

The Samaritan woman had peace about what she left behind that day at Jacob's well. We aren't told when, but at some point in the story the woman leans over and sets down her empty jar. And that's where it stayed. When she stood up she met Christ's eyes. She laid down her burdens and stood up with her hands free to receive. He had her attention all right. She wanted the water He spoke of, and she wanted to be sure both hands were free to hold it.

Then for the first time in a long time someone looked her in the eye and didn't look away in disgust. My guess is that she locked on His level gaze without feeling any condemnation. His eyes on her communicated all she had ever wanted: Love and acceptance. The about-turn in her life came when she realized despite who she was, a sinner and an outcast, He still accepted her. The revelation hit her: She didn't have to *do* anything for His love. For the first time in a very long time, she didn't have to sacrifice her body for a man's pleasure to receive *this Man's* love.

Talk about a new experience for her! She suddenly experienced *hope*. Jesus revealed himself to her (4:26), and now she knew hope. Hope for a new life, hope for restoration with her community, hope for a different future. She was a forever-after changed woman.

Hope is for *right now*. It's not only futuristic. God's Word says, "Yet this I call to mind and therefore I have hope: Because of the Lord's great love we are not consumed, for his compassions never fail. They are new every morning; great is your faithfulness" (Lamentations 3:21–23). Not consumed? Not consumed with hopelessness, not consumed with the past, not consumed with the future. Our hope in Jesus is current and existing even as you read these words.

When we lay the heavy burdens of idolatry, guilt, and emptiness at Christ's feet and then meet His eyes, we too will see hope. With our hands now free to receive, we can know and experience this hope as the encouragement to keep stepping forward toward His gaze. His eyes are locked on us, steadying our every step.

OUR HUMAN EXPERIENCE LIMITS OUR SPIRIT EXPERIENCE.

"Hope does not disappoint us" (Romans 5:5). We have all hoped for something. I've hoped for good weather on a vacation, or a letter from a friend, or a good report from the doctor. This isn't the same as the hope we have in God. Once again our human experience limits our Spirit experience.

Isaiah 40:31 offers this promise: "Those who hope in the Lord will renew their strength." Our godly hope isn't about what will happen to or around us. Godly hope is in who God is. It's transferring our limited understanding or desires to His limitless provision. That's why our strength is daily renewed by hoping in

God, because if we take the burden of hope off of ourselves or other people, it frees up and releases an inner strength.

Let me relay a story to help explain this concept of transferring hope to the Lord.

Several summers ago my family and I took our motorboat out for a spin on a lake near our home. The hourglass-shaped lake has a small, uninhabited island near the narrowest part of the water body, and it's a favorite place for motorists to buzz around fast. Which is exactly what we were doing, when suddenly into our view came a canoe, heavily weighted with four adults paddling hard away from the island toward the mainland. We slowed our boat, but not before our wake waves washed over the gunnels of the canoe. With dismay we watched it bob, tip precariously, take on water, and tip more. At that moment when we thought for sure the canoe was going to flip, we realized the people on board were friends of ours. Oh dear! We crept our motorboat up to the side of the canoe, trying not to create any more wake. Sheepishly apologizing, we grabbed the bags they tossed to us, then gingerly helped one of our friends out of the canoe. Their boat stabilized, and we motored our passenger to shore.

I learned something. A transfer needed to take place for stability to occur. Our friends had diminishing hope in their little overweighted craft. But once some of the weight was transferred to our bigger, more stable craft, they regained their hope for a safe return to land.

So it is with our hope in the Lord. We have to transfer our hope from ourselves and onto Him. If our hope stays anchored on ourselves or others, we will be disappointed. "Hope deferred makes the heart sick," according to Proverbs 13:12. In other words, misplaced hope will break our hearts.

The Lord is the only One who can carry the hope we need to

make it through the deep waters of trying situations. Our hope is *in* God and in His Word. Our hope is stored by Him, carried by Him, and is safe in Him. Psalm 119:147 confirms this: "I have put my hope in your word." *Put* it? That is, removed it from me, transferred it to Him, and left it with Him.

The word *hope* speaks to the future too. "There is surely a future hope for you and your hope will not be cut off" (Proverbs 23:18). The future hope we have in Christ is free of burdens and full of promises. It is not the kind of hope that disappears when we arrive at a certain place. No, hope is continually renewed. It is not "cut off" because it is never used up. Like a starfish that regenerates an arm if one is severed, so is our hope. It regenerates itself when it is directed vertically toward God and His Word, not laterally toward us.

> IF OUR HOPE STAYS ANCHORED ON OURSELVES OR OTHERS, WE WILL BE DISAPPOINTED.

There's even more good news about hope: it's God's hope in us. When we've placed our hope in Him, He has renewed hope for us.

This message of hope entrusted to us comes in the form of our gifts. God wants us to use these gifts to further His kingdom. Our salvation and what He has done for us is not exclusive. Though we are on a singular journey, being filled with His Living Water and drawing closer to Him each day, He longs for us to invite others along too. God is not willing that anyone should not know Him personally.

When our friend the Samaritan woman made her headlong run back to town, Jesus stayed where He was. He didn't follow her. Rather, He entrusted her to carry the message of hope to town, where her words would inspire the very people who had scorned her only hours before. She encouraged them to take their own journey to the well. Hope was waiting for them. The hope of Living Water to fill their parched souls.

That same hope is waiting for us. As is peace and the thirst-quenching Living Water of Christ that fills all the empty places in our souls. Meeting Jesus at this well is where we will find true satisfaction.

Draw Near to Him:

Have you carried idols to the well where Christ is waiting for you? Ask the Lord to search your heart and bring to mind any idol or burden that you need to confess. Write them down, then cross off each one as you choose to lay it at Christ's feet.

Drink From His Cup:

"The Lord will guide you always; he will satisfy your needs in a sun-scorched land and will strengthen your frame. You will be like a well-watered garden, like a spring whose waters never fail" (Isaiah 58:11).

Part Two

REFLECT ON THE
WATER

THE INVALID'S STORY
AT THE POOL OF BETHESDA

John 5:1–15

Some time later, Jesus went up to Jerusalem for a feast of the Jews. Now there is in Jerusalem near the Sheep Gate a pool, which in Aramaic is called Bethesda and which is surrounded by five covered colonnades. Here a great number of disabled people used to lie—the blind, the lame, the paralyzed. One who was there had been an invalid for thirty-eight years. When Jesus saw him lying there and learned that he had been in this condition for a long time, he asked him, "Do you want to get well?"

"Sir," the invalid replied, "I have no one to help me into the pool when the water is stirred. When I try to get in, someone goes down ahead of me."

Then Jesus said to him, "Get up! Pick up your mat and walk." At once the man was cured; he picked up his mat and walked.

The day on which this took place was a Sabbath, and so the Jews said to the man who had been healed, "It is the Sabbath; the law forbids you to carry your mat."

But he replied, "The man who made me well said to me, 'Pick up your mat and walk.'"

So they asked him, "Who is this fellow who told you to pick it up and walk?"

The man who was healed had no idea who it was, for Jesus had slipped away into the crowd that was there.

Later Jesus found him at the temple and said to him, "See, you are well again. Stop sinning or something worse may happen to you." The man went away and told the Jews that it was Jesus who had made him well.

CHAPTER FOUR

HANDPICKED FAITH

I was always picked last. As a knock-kneed, tall but scrawny grade-school child, playground team sports made me cringe. A heavy little girl named Ellen and I toed the dusty ground, hands behind our backs, as all the other kids were picked first for games because they could run fast, or kick the ball hard, or bully the other kids around. By the time everyone else was picked, one of the two team captains would say something like "Oh, all right, I *suppose* I'll take her," pointing a finger in my direction. Then he or she would say, "Just stay out of the way and don't mess up!" Desperate to prove myself worthy—I entered the game with my heart out of beat with my breath and feeling dizzy—I tried to do my best. But my best always seemed to be an uncoordinated and badly misplaced kick or hit.

The pattern continued into high school, where, because I was tall, I joined the basketball team, but I embarrassed my teammates and myself in my first game playing starting center. I jumped too late for the tip-off and the ball was already in the other team's hands by the time my feet hit the floor. I was never asked to start again.

Maybe this is why to this day I don't like team sports. It's not the sports I have an issue with, it's the team part that intimidates me.

That is why, I believe, the Lord has called me repeatedly to be part of teams for His work. Since by nature my preference is to work independently, He has insisted that I learn to work in groups. Small groups and larger groups, as a follower and as a leader, He has put me in all sorts of team experiences because He wants to use my strengths in these positions, but even more, He wants to see my weaknesses strengthened.

A number of years ago I began to understand something about why the Lord put me on various teams. It was for more than my usefulness to the cause. He chose me because I would be faithful to Him above all else. He was *choosing me first*.

What a revelation. I wasn't His second, third, or fourth choice. I wasn't asked to serve on the second string in God's big game plan. I was asked to be a part of different teams because I had value as a player. Because my skills were necessary to the task—I not only was needed, I was *wanted*.

Matthew 22:14 states, "Many are invited, but few are chosen." In other words, all of mankind is invited to join in the Christian life, but few of us are chosen to be part of God's team. Christ's invitation to come join the team of His followers is open to everyone. Some hear the invitation but don't respond. Others show up but don't want to join. Then there are those who think they want to join in but realize there are some rules to follow and ultimately walk away from the invitation.

But then there are the stayers—you and me. We are the ones who innately know what a privilege it is to be asked and then *chosen*. The ones chosen are willing and ready to be a part of a team that is coordinated and unified to work toward God's purposes.

In the dusty playground in my mind, I can see the hand of God outstretched toward me, with other people standing all around, and His gentle words saying, "I choose *you*. I want you on My team."

CHOSEN AND SET APART

How we answer a vital question determines what starting position we'll hold on God's team.

His question? "Do you want to get well?" (John 5:6).

This is what Jesus posed to the invalid at the pool of Bethesda. Jesus singled him out from all the other sick and diseased, just as He singles us out.

Why does He ask this? We'll be of no use to the team if we don't want to be well. He needs us spiritually fit and of sound mind to be in starting places for Him.

> HE NEEDS US SPIRITUALLY FIT AND OF SOUND MIND TO BE IN STARTING PLACES FOR HIM.

God's plan for our lives is twofold. (1) He wants a one-on-one love-relationship with us; and (2) He wants us to live out His love to others. After all, that's His second greatest commandment, "Love your neighbor" (Mark 12:31). That's the point of the team.

Everyone has value and a starting position. The invalid at the pool wasn't chosen for his physical abilities—he had few. It wasn't for his youth either; he'd already been confined there for thirty-eight years. Nor was he chosen for his cheery spirit—he actually was full of excuses: " 'Sir,' the invalid replied, 'I have no one to help me into the pool when the water is stirred. While I am trying to get in, someone else goes down ahead of me'" (John 5:7). He blamed his limitations and those around him for his situation.

> HE IS SELECTING US AS TEAM PARTNERS WITH HIM BECAUSE HE KNOWS SOMETHING OF VALUE LIES WITHIN US.

Jesus frequently used an economy of words, but there seems to be a depth of unasked questions in his query "Do you want to get well?" He might have meant, "You've been sitting here in your poverty and self-pity for thirty-eight years! Are you sure you *want* to get well? Are you sure leaving all you've known and are familiar with—begging, depending on others for your food, feeling sorry for yourself—is what you want? Because if you are sure you want to be well, I can assure you that life will actually be harder apart from what you've always known. You'll have to work. You'll have to be responsible. You'll have to take care of yourself."

The exchange really begs the question *Is this the kind of individual Jesus would choose?* Jesus looked past what *we see* as limitations and inferiorities and saw a different man. He saw faith, obedience, and an ability to talk.

Even though the invalid felt self-pity about not getting to the pool for thirty-eight years straight, he had *faith* that if he did make it to the pool, he would be healed. He showed *obedience* in immediately standing up when Jesus told him to—which, of course, Jesus knew he would. And after he was healed, when asked about why he was illegally carrying his mat on the Sabbath, he *spoke* of his Healer. Faith, obedience, and his voice were the reasons this particular man was chosen.

Likewise, He is picking us out from the crowd, selecting us as team partners with Him because He knows something of *value* lies within us.

CHOSEN FOR A VALUABLE PURPOSE

John 15:16 says, "You did not choose me, but I chose you . . . to go and bear fruit—fruit that will last." Inside each of us resides the value of fruitful lives. Part of His purpose for us is to individually bear His fruit that will then nourish other people on the team—our Christian brothers and sisters.

When Jesus chooses us from all the others around us who may appear to be more qualified, He sees something in us we may not even be aware of. Potential fruit. When He asks us, "Do you want to get well?" He's really asking, "Do you want to bear fruit that will last?" Do you want to *get well* and *be well* and *stay well* so your fruit doesn't have a shelf life but will go on to nourish others?

He has invested attributes in us that others may not yet see are the very qualities He needs to bring about His purposes. He points to you or to me and says, "Yes, I need one just like her."

> HE POINTS TO YOU OR TO ME AND SAYS, "YES, I NEED ONE JUST LIKE HER."

BELONGING

Jesus is the initiator of our souls. As we've seen, He initiated conversations with both the Samaritan woman and the lame man. He wants us to be in a love-relationship with Him. He wants us to know we belong to Him and His family. Even the Lord won't be able to satisfy our thirst for Him if we aren't fully and unabashedly confident that He loves us, He chooses us, and we belong to Him.

We all have a need to belong to something. That's why gangs fill a void in young people's lives, why groupies follow music bands, and why we join interest-oriented groups. We need to know someone values our presence.

Belonging to a group can go awry, however, when we follow a crowd that threatens our identity of belonging to Christ. Don't believe it doesn't happen in Christian groups. We see it in church splits and denominational differences far too frequently.

I know the story of a church where the congregation suffered a severe split when one influential member left the body in anger and hurt feelings over being wrongly accused of something. A number of people followed. Why did they follow? In part, it was because the person had social connections and influence among this select group. But more interesting, the group that followed the offended member also had similar patterns of hurt in their own lives. They could identify with how the angry person was feeling, so they followed what felt familiar.

This is the danger: We must be diligent not to change whom we identify with in order to follow our need to belong. Following *people* is dangerous when we do so because we see ourselves in them, think of ourselves as an extension of them, or fear living outside of their group. Christians involved in public ministries have to be extremely careful to always point people toward Christ and not their own ministry. The ministry of a Christian can't save anyone. Only Christ can do this.

We need to keep our identity in Christ and in Christ alone. Knowing we are chosen by Him and belong to Him are the qualifiers in following any group or belonging to any team. His team should always feel the most familiar and therefore be the one we want to belong to.

The invalid at the Pool of Bethesda was in a very familiar place—thirty-eight years worth of familiar. All around him were illness, disease, pain, and deformity. He identified with these people. This life was probably all he had ever known. Yet the Scripture implies that he was lonely. "I have no one to help me," he said when Jesus asked him about getting well (John 5:7). How lonely to belong to a group you don't want to be a part of but have no choice about.

We can feel lonely in our infirmities whether they are physical, emotional, or spiritual. Even if we know of other people who have similar problems, we feel lonely because no one else's experience is quite like ours. What we need is to feel confident in belonging to a group that has deeper ties than commonality of circumstances. Psalm 68:6 promises, "God sets the lonely in families." How reassuring! This is the family of God. In His family, not only will we find people with similar problems, but we'll find people who can offer their past experiences as witness to the successful growth of fruit in their lives. That's the kind of family He sets us in: supportive, understanding, encouraging, and loving.

Jesus says, "I have chosen you out of this world" (John 15:19). When we accept Christ's free gift of salvation, we no longer belong to the "world." This doesn't necessarily mean "world" as in "worldliness" or sin, though that's part of it. More important, this passage means that when Christ chooses us we become part of a new group, or a new "world." This world is the family He gives us in our brothers and sisters and mothers and fathers in Christ.

LIVING IN WELLNESS

When we belong to God's family, we are beckoned by Christ to live a new life: a life that leaves behind the darkness of sin and distress and those things that cannot satisfy our thirst for Him.

Yet we have to be willing to *move* in order to leave behind those other things. Christ is asking us: are we willing to move into a new place?

For the man at the pool, this new "place" was figurative as well as literal. Jesus was asking more than whether he wanted to *get well*. He was also asking if he wanted to *be well*, i.e., did he want to live in wellness?

> OUR THIRST FOR GOD WILL NEVER BE QUENCHED IF WE DON'T WANT TO BE WELL AND STAY IN WELLNESS.

When God chooses us, we may not be fit for the team He has in mind for us. But remember, He chooses us because He knows there is potential fruit in our lives. Are we willing to *bear* fruit, similar to the labor of bearing a child? All He needs from us is a willing heart to get well and to stay well. Our thirst for God will never be quenched if we don't want to be well and stay in wellness.

Staying well is partly keeping out of sin—not deliberately sinning. But it also means choosing health. Let's face it, we make compromises that may not be blatant sin yet still corrode our spiritual, emotional, or physical health.

For example, I can choose to stay up too late at night, which then makes me oversleep, be cranky at my family in the morning, be late getting the children to school, and feel sleepy when I sit down to work. All those consequences result from one little "innocent" choice! Though the choice itself isn't a sin, the consequences lead me to teeter on the edge of sin.

When we answer *yes* to being and staying well, our responsibility then lies in choosing to make the right choices in order to stay healthy. Jesus has gone on

> HE CHOSE US ONCE. THAT IS
>
> ALL THAT IS NEEDED.

ahead, making plans for us; He doesn't want to keep returning to our own pools of Bethesda to remind us that He already chose us. He chose us once. That is all that is needed.

OUR CHOICE OF DILIGENCE

Have you ever set your heart on something? I have. From small things like setting my heart on maple walnut ice cream for dessert, to life choices such as setting my heart on keeping my marriage vows—these are things I've purposed in my heart to do. Colossians 3:1 says, "Set your hearts on things above." In other words, our hearts should be firmly attached to godly things.

Over fifteen years ago Peter, my husband, poured the concrete floor in our barn. As the thick, gray liquid funneled down the chute from the concrete truck onto the ground, he worked fast and diligently to smooth it all out before it "set up." Once it had hardened, it was permanently set in place. Even now nothing but a jackhammer will remove it. Similarly, when we "set" our heart on godly, heavenly things nothing should be able to move it. Keep in mind, this is different than a hardened heart so often spoken of in the Bible. A hardened heart is one that is made of stone and is impenetrable to God's Word. A "set" heart means it is steadfast in keeping its intent.

We have to set our hearts diligently to stay well. We have to choose to follow the way that will keep us in health. That way is the path of righteousness that the Bible speaks of. "I have chosen the way of truth; I have set my heart on your laws" (Psalm 119:30).

> IN HIS GRACE AND MERCY HE LOVINGLY HELPS US TO LIVE OUT THAT WHICH WE COMMIT TO DOING.

Is it hard work? You bet. Is it worth the work? Of course. Is the Lord leaving us alone in this hard choice? No. Psalm 119:173 asks, "May your hand be ready to help me, for I have chosen your precepts." When we make the choice to live by the Lord's precepts, or His Word, He is ready to indeed help us live out that choice. He doesn't want to see us fail. Rather, He is the God of success stories. In His grace and mercy He lovingly helps us to live out that which we commit to doing.

The Israelites were acquainted with God's long-suffering patience with their disobedience. They finally were getting the hang of full obedience when they found themselves at the Jordan River's edge, ready to cross into the long-ago-promised Promised Land. Here Moses gives them clear, distinct direction about being diligent in following God's commands. He spoke to their insecurities and fears about not knowing what the Lord wanted them to do but assured them the Lord's direction would be clear to them. Here's part of his discourse.

> Now what I am commanding you today is not too diffi-
> cult for you or beyond your reach. It is not up in heaven, so
> that you have to ask, "Who will ascend into heaven to get it
> and proclaim it to us so we may obey it?" Nor is it beyond

the sea, so that you have to ask, "Who will cross the sea to get it and proclaim it to us so we may obey it?" No, the word is very near you; it is in your mouth and in your heart so you may obey it. (Deuteronomy 30:11–14)

This is a loaded message to the people! Moses knew their propensity to try to make excuses and blame all sorts of other factors for not listening to and obeying God. He knew their past history—he'd lived it right along with them. He was warning them, saying, "Listen, people! There are no excuses here for not obeying God's commands. You can't say you don't know them. You can't try to pretend someone has to go find them for you. They are right here, right now, right in your heart."

And do you know what? It's no different for us. When we've decided we want to know the Lord more deeply in a love-relationship and have Him alone satisfy our thirst, the answers are right in our hearts and on the tips of

> OUR THIRST CAN'T BE QUENCHED IF WE AREN'T DRINKING FROM THE WELL OF GOD'S WORD.

our tongues. God invests His Word in us and He will faithfully bring it to mind when our hearts are pure toward His purposes. As Moses said to the Israelites, we don't need to go somewhere else or look to other places for revelation.

We only need to look in our Bibles. God's Word is living and it is for today. All we have to do is ask with a sincere heart to see things and know things in the Bible that He wants us to know and live by. Psalm 119:18 says, "Open my eyes that I may see wonderful things in your law." That's a prayer for revelation. When diligently and sincerely prayed, God will be faithful to reveal things in His Word for you personally.

When we choose to accept the Lord's choice of us for His team, we have a responsibility to know what His rules are. The rules are in His Word. They are guidelines for living a righteous life, the kind of life we are thirsting for to know God more intimately. Our thirst can't be quenched if we aren't drinking from the well of God's Word.

> WHEN WE CHOOSE TO LIVE ON GOD'S TEAM AND LIVE BY HIS WORD, WE ARE CHOOSING LIFE.

Near the end of Moses' instructions to the Israelites, he says, "I have set before you life and death, blessings and curses. Now choose life, so that you and your children may live" (Deuteronomy 30:19). For them, crossing the Jordan River into the Promised Land meant they were crossing into life. Not only was the Promised Land a living land of provision for their needs, but it was also a land alive with God's presence.

We too stand at the crossroads of life and death. Life lies before us as we sign on with God's team. Death of the "old man" and the things that don't satisfy us lay behind us in the wilderness.

When we choose to live on God's team and live by His Word, we are choosing life. Not only eternal life in heaven but also a "stay-well" life on earth. Choosing to live by God's Word means you've answered yes to the question posed to the invalid at the Pool of Bethesda: "Do you want to get well?"

IS YOUR HEART STIRRED?

Some translations of the Bible tell about the stirring of the water at the pool at Bethesda. *The New King James Version* says,

"For an angel went down at a certain time into the pool and stirred up the water; then whoever stepped in first, after the stirring of the water, was made well of whatever disease he had" (John 5:4).

When the water was stirred, the invalids wanted to take action. It made them want to move, to respond to what they saw and felt.

That's how we need to feel about the stirrings in our hearts. Just as the diseased people were alert to the water and ready to move into it, we too need to be alert to the Spirit's "stirring" and be ready to move with it.

What is a stirring? It's a moving in our spirit, usually prompted by the Holy Spirit. It's a feeling of impetus to take action. It can be a small quickening in our hearts to do something, or it can feel like a giant push to put our feet in motion.

Let me give you an example of what I mean. I had been praying for the Lord to show me any parts of my heart that weren't fully turned toward Him. One night I had a dream. In my dream, my son and several of his friends were at some sort of large lodge. It was time for my son and me to leave and to take home two of his friends. My son and one friend were ready to go, but I couldn't seem to locate the other one. I thought I caught glimpses of him in the basement of one of the buildings, yet I was certain he was lost. In my dream, my irritation and annoyance at him kept growing until I was yelling at the other children to try to find him.

When I woke up, the Lord spoke to my heart. I felt stirred by a very big implication. The Lord showed me that while I was irritated at the lost little boy, I had no concern for his *lost soul*. I was more irritated than concerned. God showed me just how shallow I was: I cared more about the little boy's physical lostness than his spiritual lostness.

This stirring in my heart wasn't about the little boy (though I can assure you I started praying for him); it was about my lack of concern for all the lost souls with which I come in contact. The Lord showed me how my irritation at people was winning out over my concern for them. This was a *big* stirring in my heart to begin to pray for a true love and concern for people and for their souls.

When God asks us to do something for Him, He wants us to take action now. That doesn't mean if He tells us to go to the mission field, we should pack our bags tonight. There's usually a training process that needs to take place. But the first and best and most immediate reaction we can take in response to God's stirring our hearts is to affirm it with prayer.

Psalm 45:1 reflects, "My heart is stirred by a noble theme." What's a "noble theme"? Second Timothy 2:21 assures us that we will be "instrument[s] for noble purposes, made holy, useful to the Master and prepared to do any good work." Noble purposes and themes are those things of God that He wants our hearts to know and act on.

Our Lord is a good coach. He chooses us. He instructs us about our part in His plan, He prepares us for action, and He stirs our hearts with a knowledge and passion to go and do and bear His good fruit.

Draw Near to Him:

How long have you been gazing at the Living Water of Christ and yet have so many excuses as to why you haven't moved any closer? His question to you is: "Do you want to get well and stay well?" If your answer is yes, then you've agreed to His request for you to be part of His team.

Drink From His Cup:

"We constantly pray for you, that our God may count you worthy of his calling, and that by his power he may fulfill every good purpose of yours and every act prompted by your faith. We pray this so that the name of our Lord Jesus may be glorified in you, and you in Him" (2 Thessalonians 1:11–12).

CHAPTER FIVE

PICKUP FAITH

My sister's two children, ages six and seven, were playing on the lawn one summer day when she witnessed an interesting exchange. The children commandeered the family canoe on the grass and took turns sitting in the boat pretending to paddle. But as siblings often do, the play dissolved into bickering, and before long they argued about whose turn it was to sit in the canoe and paddle. The seven-year-old tugged and pushed the canoe while the six-year-old sat in it. Whining and fighting escalated until their mom watched the younger child wield the paddle and demand of his sister, "Hey! Paddle your own canoe!"

Out of the mouths of babes indeed come some profound words! *Don't mess with my canoe; mess with your own.*

My sister's story reminded me of how often we try to "paddle" everyone else's "canoes." Paddling your own canoe means knowing which canoe is yours, taking responsibility for it, and equally important, knowing which canoe is *not* yours.

Of course, I'm not talking about literal boats here. I'm talking about those areas in our lives that we need to be responsible for as well as those areas in others' lives for which we are not responsible. What areas? Family, money, jobs, ministry, the home, etc.

While on this thirst-quenching journey in our love-relationship with Jesus, we can't try to drag along everyone else's "canoes." We are only responsible for our own.

This is, I believe, part of what Jesus implied when He told the invalid: "Pick up your mat and walk." Pick up whose mat? His *own* mat. Jesus was saying to him, and us, be responsible for your own mat.

Why couldn't someone else, or even Jesus, pick it up for him? Because the man had to be responsible for that one thing, that one area of his life. Actually, the area was *faith*. The mat parallels the man's faith. When Jesus told him to pick up his mat, He was saying, "Pick up your *faith*. It's been right under you all this time. Now I want you to pick it up, carry it with you, and let others see it."

> WHEN JESUS TOLD HIM
> TO PICK UP HIS MAT,
> HE WAS SAYING,
> "PICK UP YOUR FAITH."

Now that's a call to being responsible for one's own canoe!

But let's back up for a minute and think about why the man had been lying on his faith for all those years.

TRAINING GROUNDS

The crippled man learned some hard lessons while lying on that hard mat and ground for thirty-eight years. It was a time of training for what was to come.

We all have training times in our lives. They may feel as dry as the forty-year wilderness hike of the Israelites, or as short as a lesson in patience for a change in a situation. Each training situation is a time of preparation. It's training for something else.

I've often felt I was standing on a training ground when the Lord was in the process of teaching me something. We don't come into our work for the Lord fully skilled for whatever task He is calling us to. We have to be trained. As author and speaker Joyce Meyer is fond of saying, "We don't start at the finish line!"

Think about farmers who for years turn over the same patches of ground: tilling, sowing, and harvesting. Each year they are faced with an unknown yield from the labor. A good year produces a good harvest, and they are ready to invest in more land to produce an even bigger crop the next year. But a poorly producing year can literally break their business of farming. They just have to doggedly go back to the same ground they've tilled for so many years and pray that the next year is better.

When we find ourselves continuously tilling the same training ground over and over, we often get discouraged. Until we can go out and re-till what we've done hundreds of times before and *not* feel discouraged, only then can we move on to the next piece of "land."

It doesn't seem likely that God will move us out of a situation about which we have complained nonstop. If we ask the Lord to change the situation or change our perspective, then He can indeed do one or both. That's the victory on the new "land" He's waiting for us to claim.

For many years I complained about the small size of my house. My whole family felt desperate for more space, yet we loved the location of our home: a mountain right outside our windows, fields and pastures, a barn we'd built ourselves, a stream in the narrow valley between the fields. How could we leave such beauty? We felt torn—leave what we loved or "suffer" in the small space.

I finally realized I was concentrating on the wrong view. I decided to stop complaining. I found things I could be thankful for. Initially it seemed silly to thank God that I could vacuum the whole downstairs of our house from one outlet, but I persevered through all sorts of things about which I could feel grateful. Once I started looking for the positives, my perspective really did change—permanently.

The discouragement of my too-small house was a training ground for me. My start of grasping-at-straws-thankfulness grew into true gratitude. On this new victory ground of gratitude God then opened a door for us to renovate and build an addition. I'm convinced that addition would not have been possible if I had continued complaining in my discouraged heart.

The Lord wants to *give us* the next victory. He wants us to walk through the land of discouragement and into the Promised Land of His faithfulness. God is not a God of withholding. His nature is to give. But He can't give us what's *next* until we accept what is for *now*.

Our training grounds can also be times of affliction. Isaiah tells us the "bread of adversity and the water of affliction" are like teachers to us (30:20). Through difficult and disappointing experiences, we

CHARACTER-BUILDING EXPERIENCES MOLD US INTO CHRISTLIKE EXAMPLES.

are taught something. Not the least of which is character. Who we are and who God wants us to be are molded from times of affliction. Character-building experiences mold us into Christlike examples.

Psalm 119 also talks about affliction being our heart teacher. It implies we can even be *thankful* for the afflictions. "Before I was afflicted I went astray, but now I obey your word" and "It was good for me to be afflicted so that I might learn your decrees" (67, 71). Sometimes the point of the affliction may be to provoke a thirst for a deeper love-relationship with Christ.

GOING DOWN BEFORE GOING UP

Jesus spent thirty years of training before the fulfillment of His three-year ministry. That's a ratio of ten years to one. Then He "descended" into hell for three wretched days to suffer the affliction of our human sin condition so we wouldn't have to.

> IN THE VALLEYS WE ARE STRIPPED OF THE "THINGS" WE THINK MAKE US READY FOR THE MOUNTAINTOPS.

Joseph too proved himself a trustworthy trainee on God's training ground through the injustices of his life. (See Genesis 37–50.) For thirteen years he lived in forced slavery, then found himself jailed after a wrongful accusation against him. All this ground had to be covered before he could come into the fulfillment of God's promise for him: a position of great authority in Pharaoh's house.

Why mention these excessive times of training? Because sometimes we have to go *down* before we go *up*. Jesus came down from heaven before He was permanently seated at God's right hand. After thirty-three years on earth He went down into hell before He ascended to heaven. Joseph went down into a pit and then into jail before he came up to a higher status in Pharaoh's house.

Sound familiar? There are going to be times when we tread

through valleys as the Lord prepares us for the mountaintops. Those valleys shape our character, test our faith, and cement our love-relationship with the Lord as our One and only source of thirst-quenching and life-giving strength.

In the valleys we are stripped of the "things" we think make us ready for the mountaintops. The Lord can't use us in our own strength. We may feel ready for lots of responsibility because we are "good" at administering or skilled in a particular area. But if we rely on our own strength we won't have the supernatural *power* that the Lord wants to administer *through* us.

Let me give you a visual. We've owned both a motorboat and kayaks. On a lake close to our home, we can race in a speedboat from one end to the other in about five minutes. In our kayaks, the journey takes closer to an hour. The Lord's strength is like the motorboat. With the throttle wide open there is serious *power*. But our own strength is more like the kayaks—we can only move as fast as we can paddle. Wouldn't you rather have the force behind the multiplied horsepower of God's divine engine than the limitation of just one person's strength?

Another lesson is that our strength alone cannot *pilot* our boats. We get humanly—spiritually, emotionally, and physically—tired. We need God's navigation and His strength to keep going. We learn to become correctly dependent on the Lord's strength as we walk the training ground He requires us to pass through.

I'm reminded of Zacchaeus—"a wee little man," as a children's song chimes (see Luke 19:1–10). He may have been a shady character and small in stature but he was big on resourcefulness. Jesus eyed Zacchaeus in the branches of the sycamore tree and demanded, "Come down immediately."

This is another "going down before going up" lesson. That Zacchaeus even climbed the tree shows he had a thirst for Christ.

But he had to come down into a one-on-one relationship with Christ to have his thirst met. Jesus needed him to come down out of his self-righteous tree so He could teach the little man a few things about being in high places.

> IT'S BECAUSE HE LOVES US THAT HE CAN'T BEAR TO SEE US "LOST" IN OURSELVES.

Jesus doesn't ground us out of spite or for punishment. He said to Zacchaeus, "For the Son of Man came to seek and to save what was lost" (Luke 19:10). It's because He loves us that He can't bear to see us "lost" in ourselves. We are lost in ourselves when we are full of ourselves. Like Zacchaeus, we are lost and out on a limb when pride, self-righteousness, and dishonor control our lives.

The Lord is calling you and me down onto His training ground. That's where we need to stand in readiness to receive the thirst-quenching life He wants us to have.

A SKEPTIC IN DISGUISE

The story is told of a woman who lived near the edge of the ocean. But she had a problem. A huge hill obstructed her view of the waves and the sea. Though she could hear the crashing waves on the shore not far off, to her frustration she couldn't see them. In discontent she stewed and stewed about what she didn't have: a view of the beloved shoreline. Then one day she heard if she had faith as small as a mustard seed she could pray for the hill to move and it would move. So one moonless night she knelt before the window facing the hill and ocean beyond and began praying. She prayed and prayed and prayed straight through the dark night. The sound of the water and waves encouraged her resolve even when she felt tired and her knees ached from kneeling. Then as the morning sun brought light to her window she dared to open her eyes. And there before her was . . . the hill. She wearily got to her feet, rubbed her eyes, shook her head, and said, "See, I knew it wouldn't work."

We can't hide our skepticism from the Lord. Like the woman praying at the window, we say that we are trusting the Lord to move the hill, but we're clutching a shovel behind our backs.

This is how we sabotage our faith—by not really believing what we claim we believe. Our faith is stretched when the clock of the Lord's timing seems to need rewinding. Yet having faith means we don't need to help the Lord along. Sometimes we think a shovel will help. Our shovels are signs of skepticism about God's trustworthiness. If you've never been able to walk through a training ground to the end, then you haven't experienced God's trustworthiness.

> OUR FAITH IS STRETCHED WHEN THE CLOCK OF THE LORD'S TIMING SEEMS TO NEED REWINDING.

Can we hold in trust what God has said He would do? As hard and nail-bitingly slow as it may feel to us, His time frame, without our interruptions, truly is better than ours.

WALKING IN FAITH

We are gathering more than dust on our feet as we walk these training grounds. What are we gathering in the storehouses of our hearts along the journey? Are we picking up our faith to carry with us? Just as the invalid learned, we have to pick up our "mats" of faith to rise up and walk into God's plan.

James talks about putting feet to our faith. "Was not our ancestor Abraham considered righteous for what he did when he offered his son Isaac on the altar? You see that his faith and his actions were working together, and his faith was made complete by what he did. And the scripture was fulfilled that says, 'Abraham believed God, and it was credited to him as righteousness,' and he was called God's friend. You see that a person is justified by what he does and not by faith alone" (James 2:21–24).

Even as Abraham's hand held a sharp-edged knife to sacrifice his own son, he didn't doubt God's promise of his descendants being as numerous as the stars (Genesis 15:5). Abraham might not have planned exactly on God's provision through the ram caught by its horns in a nearby thicket. But he did plan on God fulfilling His promise. That's faith in knowing God's trustworthiness but not knowing *how,* or even second-guessing how God would prove His trust.

THE CREDIT OF RIGHTEOUSNESS

Genesis 15:6 says, "Abram believed the Lord, and he credited it to him as righteousness." Credited as righteousness? It means the correct way of thinking and acting was held in Abraham's favor. Abraham was choosing to live a righteous life, of taking God at His Word.

Living a righteous life means we believe what God says. It means we believe what the Bible says—all of it, not just the convenient and easy parts. It means we believe the promises God sets out for us. But equally important, it means we believe the consequences of not living out the words of the Lord.

This is where we get into trouble. We like to live on the promises of God—it's exciting to see how God brings His Word to fulfillment. But I think we don't truly believe there are distinct pitfalls to disobedience. We like to believe and live in God's grace, but we confuse that grace with permissiveness. We live on the edge of disobedience because we know God will forgive us. Isn't that taking advantage of the Cross? Isn't that minimizing the sacrifice of God's only Son?

When we live in such a way that God can "credit" us, because we choose to live in awe of His grace, then we are choosing righteousness. This is why when the Word says our belief is "credited to [us] as righteousness" we should want to be daily adding righteousness to our personal reserves.

LIVING A RIGHTEOUS LIFE

MEANS WE BELIEVE

WHAT GOD SAYS.

Let me give you an example of what I mean. I like to play Monopoly with my children. The game shows us a lot about our character and personalities. One of my children is a complete risk taker, spending all the money on buying properties, putting up houses and hotels, and mortgaging other properties to pay off debts. The other child is a generous player, giving away money and property on whims. I'm a fairly low-risk player. I buy property and houses, but only if I have a cash reserve. That cash reserve is usually stashed under the board. I'm never really certain how much I have, but I know there's always some under there.

This is how I feel about righteousness. I'd rather have some "stored up" from making wise choices than to deplete it all in a few bad choices. This is why God calls it *credited,* because righteousness is like a savings account. We can gain it, save it, store it up, and have it on reserve for when conflict comes our way.

SPIRITUAL ACCOUNTABILITY

Living a righteous life is taking personal responsibility for your faith walk. Like "paddling your own canoe," you alone are responsible for your faith and the nurture of it.

Too often we look outside ourselves for the faith we feel certain will be provided elsewhere. We look to spiritual "happenings" and hang our hats of faith on those instead of God himself.

I once watched a disturbing television documentary about faith healers. One couple had brought their son to a faith healing service as a last-ditch hope to cure an inoperable brain tumor. The child was dying. Doctors had said there was nothing they could do, telling the parents simply to treasure the child's last few weeks of life. The couple was young in their faith and completely hooked by the faith healer, pledging money they did not have to the ministry. The TV program showed them packing up their son in their car, driving hundreds of miles, and arriving at the faith healer's scheduled service. They brought the boy to the front of the auditorium, and the healer prayed over him as the parents looked on, weeping. Two weeks later the child was dead.

Now, before anyone thinks I'm discounting healing, I'm most certainly not. I've had healing take place in my own life—I know my Lord is capable beyond my imagination. But the comments of the grieving parents after they lost their precious child were deeply disturbing. When asked by the TV interviewer if they stopped supporting and believing in the ministry of the faith healer, they didn't hesitate to say they continued to pledge huge sums of money and watch the televised program regularly. When asked if they still had faith in the Lord as Healer they *hesitated*. They then looked at one another, shrugged their shoulders, and with little conviction said that yes, they still had faith in God.

That's the danger of ill-directed faith. Our faith cannot be in man or what we believe man can do—no matter how gifted and anointed of the Lord the person may be. Our faith is in the Lord, even when in our humanness we are disappointed.

Paul warned young Timothy to be aware of and to speak the truth against false teachers and confusing events. Paul said,

> Stay there in Ephesus so that you may command certain men not to teach false doctrines any longer nor to devote themselves to myths and endless genealogies. These promote controversies rather than God's work—which is by faith. The goal of this command is love, which comes from a pure heart and a good conscience and a sincere faith. Some have wandered away from these and turned to meaningless talk. They want to be teachers of the law, but they do not know what they are talking about or what they so confidently affirm. We know that the law is good if one uses it properly. (1 Timothy 1:3–8)

What can we learn from this? "Sincere faith" is knowing we can't explain some things, and it's okay that we can't. If we try by human terms to explain the unexplainable we diminish God. We also warp our faith. The things

IF WE TRY BY HUMAN TERMS TO EXPLAIN THE UNEXPLAINABLE WE DIMINISH GOD.

of God are frequently unexplainable. This doesn't mean we can't pray for wisdom and knowledge and understanding from the Lord—we should desire those things. But the unexplainable things we sometimes have to leave in the hands of faith.

THE BRIDGE OF FAITH

The Bible says having faith is being certain of things unseen (2 Corinthians 5:7; Hebrews 11:1).

The Israelites had faith the Promised Land was out there, somewhere.

The prophets of the Old Testament had faith they were foretelling the spiritual future of the nation of Israel—even though they would never be witness to it.

The apostles, particularly Paul, who told of Christ's second coming, had faith the Lord would appear—soon.

These were all unseen things, yet they had varying levels of faith in the future because they had experienced God's faithfulness.

Confidence, on the other hand, is only the midpoint of faith. The invalid at the pool of Bethesda had *confidence* he would be healed if another person dragged him to the pool. His confidence was in a person helping him.

But Jesus challenged him to think bigger and not to put his confidence in people. Christ essentially said, "Your faith is right here with you; your confidence shouldn't be on someone else to get you to the pool to receive your healing."

Second Corinthians 5:6 says, "Therefore we are always confident and know that as long as we are at home in the body we are away from the Lord." This reminds us that if we are secure and at ease in the body, then we aren't with the Spirit of God. The "body" has two meanings. First, it means the body of believers—other people. Second, it means our own flesh—our humanity. If we place confidence in either people or in ourselves we have diminished faith in the Lord.

So what's the difference between confidence and faith?

I'll give you a visual. Near my home is a one-hundred-year-old man-made pond that was created by damming a low-lying, swampy area. The concrete dam holds back the pond with an eight-foot spillway in the middle. A heavy timber bridge spans this open section. I've crossed this bridge on foot, on horseback, and on cross-country skis. It's a solid bridge.

I have *confidence* in the man-made bridge and the materials used to make the bridge. I have *faith* that I'll get to the other side safely. Do you see the difference? Confidence is in what is human-made, tangible, under my feet. Faith is in what's before me—the other side.

GATHERING FAITH

Chapter 3 of Ecclesiastes talks about "a season for everything." Paralleling the seasons of nature, Solomon's seasons about life each mark a beginning and an end.

The author says, "[There is] a time to scatter stones and a time to gather them." Similar to our current day, I suspect that stones or rocks could be seen as a nuisance or, conversely, as a help (3:5).

Rocky New Hampshire, where I live, is affectionately known as "The Granite State." "Affectionately known" only to those who don't have to dig out rocks and boulders and stones in order to build houses, gardens, or dig holes for fence posts. We've learned to dislike removing rocks. Yet at the same time we love to build stone walls. So the very thing we hate dislodging is used for something we enjoy. We can't have one without the other. We have to remove the scattered underground rocks to gather them again to build.

How is this similar to our faith? There is a time we have to put down—or scatter—our confidence in people. Then is the time we can pick up—or gather—our faith in God. We can't do the second until the first is done.

IT'S A LONELY JOB

Picking up faith is a lonely job. No one else can pick up our faith for us. Yes, we can be fed and encouraged and challenged in our faith by other people. But the ultimate responsibility of who is going to carry your personal faith is you. Just as the invalid at the pool learned, no one else was asked or called to carry his mat of faith. He was solely responsible.

Consider the great men and women in both the Old and New Testaments who were called by God to carry their own banners of faith: Moses, called from the desert to lead his people; Daniel, set apart as a righteous young man; David, a fearless leader and warrior; Mary, mother to the Savior of the world; Paul, an ambassador beaten for Christ.

Were these people scared? Most certainly. Did they feel alone in the call to faith? Probably. Are they so different than us? Not much.

Their stories are familiar to us. Our advantage is in knowing their stories from the beginning to the end. All they knew was the Lord's singular call on their lives to walk His training ground, carrying the faith He'd placed in them.

God's plan for His people hasn't changed. He is still calling us to tread training grounds to prepare us for an unknown future that is full of promise. All we can do is pick up our faith and walk where He directs us. The good news is the more quickly we learn from our training grounds and the more readily we obey His call, the more we'll find our thirst for Him quenched.

Draw Near to Him:

Do you feel as though you are on a training ground with the Lord? Have you picked up your faith when He has asked you to?

Ask the Lord to reveal to you any way in which you may have allowed your faith to stay scattered. Then trust Him for more righteousness in your life as you pick up your faith and stand in His promises.

Drink From His Cup:

"For in the gospel a righteousness from God is revealed, a righteousness that is by faith from first to last, just as it is written: 'The righteous will live by faith' " (Romans 1:17).

CHAPTER SIX

WILLING FAITH

There is a common denominator among children, especially preteens: dawdling. I can say to my son, "Please put on your shoes and get your backpack so we can leave for school in two minutes." Two minutes later I'll find him sitting on his bed fascinated with a piece of string. My son is not hearing impaired, he's just twelve.

I've talked with him about the importance of what we call "immediate obedience"—the need to obey right when asked. If I find him distracted and taking his time instead of doing what was asked, he'll do a heel-of-hand-to-head slap and say, "Darn! I forgot immediate obedience again!"

It takes personal discipline to learn to be obedient. It takes even more discipline to obey *immediately*. Despite the inabilities of the invalid at the pool of Bethesda, he had learned self-discipline. So when Christ told him to stand up, he didn't hesitate or make any further excuses. He stood up right away. He was immediately obedient.

We too have to learn immediate obedience to Christ's requests of us. As we are moving into a pure love-relationship with Him and learning to live a righteous life, we have to be obedient to walk the path to which Christ calls us.

We'll come to many crossroads along our journey with Him. Some may look like they are shortcuts, and we feel certain they must be the quickest, easiest route to where we need to go. Not surprisingly, though, the Lord may tell us, "No, I want you to take this path." Where He points seems to lead away from where we think we should be headed. Then we do the unthinkable: We hesitate. Those hours, days, or years of hesitation may cost us more than we'll ever know.

THE BLESSINGS OF OBEDIENCE

In immediate obedience are blessings. We make the mistake of measuring God's blessings by the size, number, and value of our material possessions. Our yardsticks are too short if we measure that way.

> WE MAKE THE MISTAKE OF MEASURING GOD'S BLESSINGS BY THE SIZE, NUMBER, AND VALUE OF OUR MATERIAL POSSESSIONS.

The true value of God's blessings in our lives is a deepened love-relationship with Him. The blessing that comes from obedience to God translates to trustworthiness and righteousness in us. And the more trustworthy we are to His call, the more He'll entrust to us.

Who wants to delay the benefits of obedience with hesitation? If we aren't obedient in the small call why would the Lord even call us to something "big"?

Once when my husband was away, as I was in the middle of doing barn chores, I felt the Lord nudge me to take my children to a local family restaurant for dinner. I knew the thought couldn't have originated in my own mind for several reasons. First, I was tired. I didn't feel like taking a shower, putting on decent clothes, and driving to a neighboring town. I'd rather stay home and fix eggs for dinner. Second, I didn't want to spend the money. We had been trying diligently to stick to a family budget. Yet it felt fairly clear in my spirit that we needed to go. I obeyed.

> OUR OBEDIENCE IS NEVER SINGULAR IN ITS RESULTS.

It was a small obedience, but I've learned small obediences are added to our righteousness credit accounts. I'm glad I went to the restaurant. While there I saw an acquaintance. She saw me too but we didn't even talk to each other. Yet what lacked in words showed in her demeanor. With spiritual eyes I saw she felt shaken by a confidence crisis. I had no idea specifically what it was, but I prayed for her anyway.

Several weeks passed before I saw her again. Once more no words passed between us, but I immediately saw a change in her. She held her shoulders straighter, her smile was broader, and the joy of the Lord shone on her face. Several more weeks passed, and then I heard about how she had become involved in a ministry. This ministry had brought her into a new level of her giftedness and a greater confidence in herself and her place in the Lord's plan.

In hindsight, I felt so privileged to have been a silent partner in praying her through her shaken confidence. It was a small obedience to go to the restaurant, but it served to remind me of all the opportunities the Lord calls us to that can have an effect in someone else's life.

Our obedience is never singular in its results. There will always be a ripple effect. The reason God calls us to do His work is to have an effect on other people, which benefits His kingdom. That's the Great Commission. "Therefore go and make disciples of all nations, baptizing them in the name of the Father and of the Son and of the Holy Spirit, and teaching them to *obey everything I have commanded you*" (Matthew 28:19–20, emphasis added). The furthering of God's kingdom lies in our obedience. What a responsibility!

FROM GLORY TO GLORY

"And we, who with unveiled faces all reflect the Lord's glory, are being transformed into his likeness with ever-increasing glory, which comes from the Lord, who is the Spirit" (2 Corinthians 3:18). We are a reflection, a mirror image, of God's glory. As we walk with Him and commune with Him and deepen our love-relationship with Him, we take on more of His likeness—not only an internal likeness within our spirit but also our external actions that reflect Him in how we conduct ourselves.

We grow from glory to glory. Like a point-to-point race, each glory we reach with Him gives us strength and hope and courage for the next glory-reaching step.

The Bible says Christ was obedient to death (Philippians 2:8). Then the very next sentence says, "Therefore God exalted him to the highest place . . . to the glory of God the Father" (9, 11). God's glory was exalted because Christ was obedient.

This is a crucial concept to understand. If we are growing into ever-increasing glory through and with Christ, then we must be as willingly obedient as He was. Growing from glory to glory in the Lord is parallel to walking from obedience to obedience. God's glory in and through us is dependent on our obedience.

Daily obediences are the stepping-stones that we use to navigate the training grounds of our lives. We step in faith from one obedience to the next. When we do, we learn that God is *always* faithful with our acts of obedience. When the Lord has asked us to do something, and we do it, of course He's going to reward us! In this divine Father-child relationship He wants to reward us for good behavior.

> GOD'S GLORY IN AND THROUGH US IS DEPENDENT ON OUR OBEDIENCE.

I learned this basic principle when my horse, now fifteen years old, was an opinionated colt. If I was working in or near the barn and he was in his stall, he'd bang the stall door with his front hoof to get my attention. If I told him to stop, he would, for about five seconds, then he'd go back to banging. If I gave him some hay he'd stop banging until he was done eating, then he'd bang again. Banging his door was not acceptable behavior. It was obnoxious, and it tore at the door. I realized I was actually rewarding his bad behavior by giving him hay to eat. He loves food, and he learned if he pestered me enough with his banging he'd get something to eat. I had to retrain him that quietly standing still would result in the reward he wanted: food. His reward only came in obedience.

Similarly, the Lord wants to give us the blessings and rewards of appropriate behavior. That behavior is basic obedience to His Word and what He tells us to do.

THE HURT OF OBEDIENCE

Obedience doesn't always feel good. As a matter of fact, it can frequently be painful. This is because our flesh—our human nature—must die to itself in order to obey the Lord. We want everything to be easy, to feel good, to be instantaneous. Our drive-through culture designed for instant gratification feeds our assumption that life should be easy.

Too often fear of loss dictates our obedience: loss of relationships, loss of material possessions, loss of self. Yet dying to self—our wants and wishes—is the only way we can promote the Lord's kingdom. As Paul wrote, "I eagerly expect and hope that I will in no way be ashamed, but will have sufficient courage so that now as always Christ will be exalted in my body, whether by life or by death. For to me, to live is Christ and to die is gain" (Philippians 1:20–21).

Psalm 15 says a righteous man who may live in God's presence is "[one] who keeps his oath even when it hurts" (v. 4). Our oath before God is to live according to His Word. But sometimes pain goes hand in hand with obedience, because each step into faith means that more of our own nature is being torn from us. Selfishness, pride, dishonesty, idolatry all must die in us and be removed from our spirits. The Lord gives us abundant opportunities to do things right, to do things the way He says, and how He says, and when He says. Fortunately He's not a three-strikes-and-you're-out God. He is indeed long-suffering. Not only does this mean He is patient, it means He suffers with us when we don't obey Him and His Word, because He so wants to bless and bless and bless us, but He can't if we haven't yet learned to obey!

THE BEGINNING OF OBEDIENCE

What exactly is the Lord asking you to do? Maybe He's telling you to quit some bad habits, like overeating or over-spending or chronic bitterness and discontent. Is He telling you to sell your home and move, or open your home to people in need? Maybe He's telling you to quit your job, or change jobs. Is it to confront someone about his or her lifestyle, or hold your tongue about a situation? Maybe He wants you to let go of a long-held dream, or He's telling you to dream farther than the nearest horizon.

How can you *know* what He's asking you to do? You can only know by listening to His Word. "The fear of the Lord is the beginning of knowledge" (Proverbs 1:7). Fearing God, offering respect to Him for who He is and His greatness, is only the *starting* point of knowledge. We will have no knowledge of what God wants us to do if we don't revere Him as God. We've minimized God with our prayers: "Lord, just . . ." as if He were promoting an athletic shoe: "Just do it, God!"

> HE'S SAYING, "I HAVE GREAT THINGS IN STORE FOR YOU; FOLLOW MY DIRECTIONS. IT'S A WONDERFUL PLAN!"

Our knowledge and understanding of what the Lord wants us to do in obedience comes from a "fear" or deep respect for Him. We have a warped idea of obedience, envisioning the Lord with a whip in one hand and a gavel in the other, issuing orders and judgment in a single sentence. We need to know He doesn't ask us to obey because He is demanding of us some terrible thing. God is asking us to obey because it's the only way He can give us the desires of our hearts.

He's saying, "I have great things in store for you; follow my directions. It's a wonderful plan!"

THE LOOK OF OBEDIENCE

God's Word is full of all His commands, laws, and precepts. These aren't suggestions of how we *might* want to live our lives. They are His holy rules for righteous living. They aren't optional according to how you feel. Obedience isn't based on feelings.

The look of obedience is found in the Ten Commandments. Every sin we suffer is born of neglect of one of the commandments. That's why God gave them. If we follow them, we will be living a life that is very close to His heart. Obeying God's laws keeps our feet in step with God's targeted plan for us.

Why are nine of the ten written in the negative? Not because God is pointing a giant finger at us and saying, "No, no, no." Rather, He is saying, "Yes, yes, yes" to everything *except* these things.

Too often we see the limitations of the Ten Commandments. He only told us ten things not to do, so everything else we are free to do! We are free to be in a safe, one-on-one, love-relationship with the Designer of the universe. We are free to love all of His creation and praise Him for it. We are free to love all of mankind with purity and find joy in human relationships. We are free to work, and work hard, for six full days. We are free to give generously. We are free to be honest and tell the truth. We are free to love where the Lord has placed us to live. We are free to have hope and courage in the situations He calls us to. When we consider the commandments as ways in which we can show our love and respect for the Lord, we see they are all simply affirming of Him, His creation, and His desire for us to have full, happy, and productive lives.

The Ten Commandments are the foundation of all other obediences to which God calls us. The Lord wants our thirst for Him to be quenched. Actually, no one wants this more than He does, because when our thirst is constantly met by Him, it means we are hand in hand, step by step in a love-relationship with Him. Disobeying any of the Ten Commandments and being in sin separates our grip from His. He can't give us His thirst-quenching presence if our hands are occupied with sin rather than empty to take hold of His cup of grace.

THE SAFETY OF OBEDIENCE

My husband and I have dug holes for fence posts and hammered rails on the posts to create pastures for my horses. Outside of the fence lines are dangerous roads, deep ditches, and poisonous plants. Within the fenced areas my horses are free to run and play and eat grass and enjoy life. Within the fence lines there is safety and, yes, a very pleasant life.

> HIS WORD TAKES THE GUESSWORK OUT OF LIFE.

The same is true for the safety we have within the boundary lines God puts in our lives. The psalmist says, "The boundary lines have fallen for me in pleasant places" (Psalm 16:6). The boundaries of the Ten Commandments are the markers for the outer limits of unacceptable behavior and actions. Inside His boundaries are the most pleasant places to abide: "I run in the paths of your commands, for you have set my heart free," and "I will walk about in freedom, for I have sought out your precepts" (Psalm 119:32, 45). There is freedom and safety in the paths, commands, and precepts of the Lord.

All of God's commands afford us knowledge of how to lead our lives. His Word takes the guesswork out of life. Isn't there great relief and freedom in knowing that nothing in how we act or choices we make need to be a guess at what's right? We aren't stabbing in the dark hoping to hit an unseen mark. No, we are armed with the light of God's Word, and we'll hit a bull's-eye every time when we follow His commands.

THE RISK OF OBEDIENCE

There's nothing worse than feeling out of control. Occasionally if I'm feeling stressed or overwhelmed about a situation I'll have nightmares about driving a car in the snow at night without headlights, or speeding along a highway with no brakes. You get the picture. Something in my life feels out of control, and my subconscious mind picks up where my conscious mind fell asleep.

And that's the risk of obedience: we feel completely out of control. Similar to my out-of-control nightmares, we have no steering, we can't see the road ahead of us, it seems to be rushing at us much too fast, and we have no way of stopping it. Whew! What a ride with the Lord! But I'd rather have the uncertainty of no personal control of my life and know the Lord is in the driver's seat than try to be certain and take over the wheel. Do you know why? Because having control of our lives is just a mirage. It's elusive, and the more we try to capture control the farther it gets from our grasp. None of us knows the number of our days, but God does. Wouldn't you rather rest your uncertain days in His hands?

No one is more concerned with your life than the Lord is— the living of your life and the length of it. This is not because He wants to dictate it but because He wants it to be useful. When we obey the Lord, we've relinquished our rights to our lives. Our lives matter most in the context of what God can do to bring about His work, His kingdom, His righteousness. This doesn't mean that God only loves us for what we accomplish. It means His accomplishments through us bring Him the most glory.

The risk of obedience also means the loss of our own identity. With what do we want to be identified? Our homes, our kids, our jobs? Or in the grander picture of God's perfect plan, would you rather be identified with Him?

Let me give you a visual. When our family goes on vacation we'll often bring a big puzzle with us. On rainy days we'll sit for hours stringing together the outer edges and then filling in the interior, trying pieces with the right size and coloring and knobs and indents, fitting them in the exact places they belong. It's frustrating and rewarding at the same time—hard because we sometimes have to stubbornly search for just the right piece, and rewarding when the puzzle starts to take on an actual picture of something recognizable.

Similarly, the Lord's plan has often been compared to a giant jigsaw puzzle. It's a puzzle that is ongoing, always being worked on, always having pieces moved into the right positions. As the pieces come together the picture starts to show itself stunning and beautiful. But there's bad news and good news. The bad news is that during our time on earth we won't see the puzzle finished. All we'll see is other pieces around us. We'll only be able to see as far as the horizon. Whereas the Lord has a bird's-eye view of how each piece holds a place with the next. The good news is that in His giant handiwork each of our pieces is crucial to the completion and beauty of the entire picture.

This is what I want to identify with: God's bigger picture. I want to be part of God's giant masterpiece that He's been stringing together since the beginning of time. Yes, there's a risk in this because we don't know where our little piece will fit into His big plan. But I'd rather not selfishly try to wedge myself in the wrong place. I'd rather, in obedience, be placed in just the right place at the right time for the fullest effect to further the Lord's kingdom plan.

The risk of obedience requires a servant's heart. A servant's heart is one that is pleased to serve. It's not done with a grudging heart or dragging feet. The servant doesn't ask of his master, "Please use me." Instead, he or she says, "How can I best promote you as King?" This needs to be our prayer of obedience. How can we best bring about the Lord's kingdom—His perfect, huge, beautiful, glorious picture?

The Lord wants our prayer to be, "Establish your kingdom in me no matter what it costs me personally." This is a prayer of personal sacrifice. It's a prayer of complete faith that the Lord's plan is the best, and the best that we could think of for ourselves is a distant second.

> THE LORD WANTS OUR PRAYER TO BE, "ESTABLISH YOUR KINGDOM IN ME NO MATTER WHAT IT COSTS ME PERSONALLY."

THE BENEFIT OF OBEDIENCE

What was the first thing the lame man did after he accepted his healing, stood up next to the pool of Bethesda, picked up his mat of faith, and walked away? He went to the temple. Why? I believe it was because he had felt deprived of spiritual fulfillment for all those years while lying on his mat. And what did he find at the temple? Christ met him there. Up until Jesus confronted him in the temple, the man professed he had no idea who had healed him. But after Christ spoke with him, the man suddenly recognized just who Jesus was. At the temple he found revelation. He went looking for spiritual fulfillment, and he found it in Christ's presence.

This is the benefit of obedience. The man was obedient to get well, stay well, get up, pick up his faith, and walk. At the end of all those obediences he found what had been lacking for so many years. His thirst for physical, emotional, and spiritual health was quenched.

Draw Near to Him:

Has obedience to the Lord's call been hard for you to follow? What is hindering your obedience to Him: fear of loss, a sense of no control, a proud heart? Ask the Lord to reveal to you any areas where you have been willfully disobedient. Pray for His grace to give you more opportunities to learn to be obedient.

Drink From His Cup:

"You are my portion, O Lord; I have promised to obey your words. . . . I have considered my ways and have turned my steps to your statutes. I will hasten and not delay to obey your commands" (Psalm 119:57, 59–60).

Part Three

PARTAKE OF
THE WATER

CHRIST'S FIRST MIRACLE: WATER TO WINE

John 2:1–11

On the third day a wedding took place at Cana in Galilee. Jesus' mother was there, and Jesus and his disciples had also been invited to the wedding. When the wine was gone, Jesus' mother said to him, "They have no more wine."

"Dear woman, why do you involve me?" Jesus replied. "My time has not yet come."

His mother said to the servants, "Do whatever he tells you."

Nearby stood six stone water jars, the kind used by the Jews for ceremonial washing, each holding from twenty to thirty gallons.

Jesus said to the servants, "Fill the jars with water"; so they filled them to the brim.

Then he told them, "Now draw some out and take it to the master of the banquet."

They did so, and the master of the banquet tasted the water that had been turned into wine. He did not realize where it had come from, though the servants who had drawn the water knew. Then he called the bridegroom aside and said, "Everyone brings out the choice wine first and then the cheaper wine after the guests have had too much to drink; but you have saved the best till now."

This, the first of his miraculous signs, Jesus performed in Cana of Galilee. He thus revealed his glory, and his disciples put their faith in him.

CHAPTER SEVEN

EMPTY VESSELS

When I was nine, my parents, my two older sisters, and I packed our Chevy van, hitched a trailer to the back, and set off north then west across Canada, then south and east back home. For eight weeks we traveled through the magnificent Canadian provinces and then under the expansive U.S. western skies. It's a journey I still carry with me over thirty years later.

In hindsight, I see how a basic principle of life dictated our every move. At each park we visited, at every evening campground, we constantly emptied or refilled something. When the gas tank was empty, we refilled it with gas. We emptied the trash before leaving the campground. The refrigerator always needed restocking. We emptied the laundry bag of dirty clothes, then filled the washer at the Laundromat, then emptied it. Empty and refill . . . over and over and over.

One day I remember waiting at a railroad crossing, and as is the habit of children, my sisters and I counted the cars as they clanged over the rails in front of us. My father asked us what we thought certain letters meant on the sides of some of the cars. I thought I was being pretty smart and quick when I answered the two letters M T scrawled in chalk on the sides of some cars meant "mountain." He asked me why the train cars would have the word *mountain* on them? I couldn't think of a good reason, so I changed my thought and said maybe the letters meant the state where the trains were bound. My dad shook his head and suggested that I try saying the two letters M and T together, fast. Okay. MT, mt, emt . . . empty! He explained how these two letters quickly told car handlers the cars were empty without having to open the doors and look inside.

Looking back, I see how this simple linguistics lesson took on a deeper meaning for me. I now understand that emptying and refilling is a principle of life, especially the Christian's life.

I've also learned that "empty" is a starting point. Most of life as we know it starts out empty. A womb is empty before conception. We fill an empty glass with water. A newly built house stands empty. An empty picture frame is filled with a photo. Even a new calendar is empty of personal marks of ownership. It takes our wants and wishes and desires to fill the emptiness with the marks of ourselves.

The expanse of God's creation started empty too. "In the beginning God created the heavens and the earth. Now the earth was formless and empty . . ." (Genesis 1:1–2). The world as we know it started empty. It took the voice of God to fill the space.

This is where we begin too: empty. Not that we're mindless and void of feelings and substance. But we are empty of the spirit of God until we ask Him to come in and fill our souls. This is why mankind has a perpetual thirst for the things of God. Our souls thirst for God because they are empty of His Living Water.

EMPTINESS = POTENTIAL

Starting empty means we are full of potential. We talked in the earlier chapters about coming to the Lord empty of ourselves and our dreams and hopes and hurts and expectations. So coming to Him empty means we are actually halfway to being filled! Does my math not compute? If we are empty of ourselves and ready and willing to be refilled with the things of the Lord, little time is needed to weed out and create the empty spaces. The time is cut in half if we start out empty.

When Jesus changed the water to wine, the water jars stood empty to start with. Being empty meant they were halfway to their usefulness for

> STARTING EMPTY MEANS WE ARE FULL OF POTENTIAL.

Christ's purposes. It's the same with us. Being empty of ourselves means we are halfway to being useful for Christ's kingdom. In the previous chapter we looked at asking the Lord not to "use me" but to "establish your kingdom in me." Being empty first means He can, indeed, establish His kingdom in us because we've made room for His kingdom.

A PREPARED GARDEN

I like to garden, or rather I like the benefit of my garden. I like to pick colorful flowers for the dining room table. I like to cook fresh vegetables or make muffins from just-picked blueberries. But the garden needs to start empty of all last year's debris before I can hope for a harvest. And that's the part I don't enjoy. Yet if I don't pull up all the plants from the past year before I plant, or if I try to press seeds in between weeds, I can't hope for much of a harvest. Similarly, we have to empty ourselves in faith, and trust the Lord to plant and bring a harvest in our lives.

An even greater step of faith is to ask the Lord to prune and weed the dead and useless areas of our lives. Extra little stems or branches on a young plant are called suckers, because they pull vital nutrients away from the upward stalk growth. The suckers need to be pinched off. My grandfather, an avid gardener, always said of this pinching process, "It only hurts for a minute."

In our lives, these "suckers" of sin need to be pinched off to encourage our full potential for growth. Remember, if we are empty of the things in our lives that are not thirst-quenchers, then we are full of potential to receive the things of God that *will* quench our thirst.

Asking the Lord to prune us in this way hurts! But in faith we know it is what will benefit Him—and us—the most. Hebrews 12:11 reminds us of why we need to be pruned: "No discipline seems pleasant at the time, but painful. Later on, however, it produces a harvest of righteousness and peace for those who have been trained by it."

> HE DISCIPLINES US BECAUSE WE ARE CHILDREN IN NEED OF DIRECTION AND BOUNDARIES.

God's discipline is pruning. The Lord disciplines us, and yes, though He is a loving and patient and gracious God, He is also a parent. He disciplines us because we are children in need of direction and boundaries. A subtle meaning of this verse also reminds us that it's not only God's job to discipline us. Just as any parent hopes, He would like us to become less dependent on Him for discipline. If we learn to be self-disciplined, there is less painful pruning required. We need to learn to pinch off our own "suckers," so to speak.

Acting with self-discipline means we have no claim to "self."

The Lord calls himself the Great I Am. If He is the one and only "I Am," it means that I, Elizabeth, am *not*. The disciplined life the Lord wants us to live is a life for Him and His purposes, not our own.

Self-discipline means we choose to lead a righteous life. It means doing the right thing even when it hurts, even when it means we are humbled, even if it means someone may gloat. It means emptying ourselves of our will to bring a greater benefit to others.

GOOD SOIL

Throughout God's Word are analogies of planting and sowing and harvesting. Within these stories our assigned identities change: Sometimes we are His field, other times we are the sowers, and still other times the harvesters. In each case we are entrusted with seed. That seed is His Word. But the seed of His Word can only thrive in the empty, ready places of our lives, because there it is given the best opportunity to grow through faithful watering and nurture.

Jesus spoke in parables because they are parallels to our lives. Parables are word pictures that the men and women of the New Testament could understand as fishermen, farmers, and merchants.

When He spoke of the parable of the sower, He explained that what is sown—or scattered as seed—is the Word of God (see Matthew 13:1–23). But then one of four things happens to the Word: it falls on a path (where it is snatched up by birds of prey); it's sown on rocky places (where it cannot grow a root); it's sown among thorns (where it gets strangled); or it's sown on good soil (where it produces an abundant harvest). A missionary visiting my church noted this story communicates only a 25 percent success rate. He also noted we are the sowers as well as the receivers of the Word. We therefore have a dual purpose: to receive the Word and to spread it as sowers.

As sowers we have two basic planting grounds: our own fields in our own hearts and those fields of service where God directs us. If there is only a 25 percent success rate, is this true of our own hearts too? I believe, sadly, it is.

My question of the sower has always been "What's wrong with him?" Why is he scattering seed on places where there's so little chance of growth? Doesn't he know to prepare the ground ahead of time and create empty spaces to give the seed its best opportunity? Isn't that wasteful of 75 percent of his seed and effort? If *we* are the sowers, as God says we are, what does this say about us?

In our dual purpose as noted above, we are also the receivers (the ground) of the seed (the Word). We assume we are the 25 percent—the "good soil." But our confidence in that 25 percent needs to be drawn from knowing that the path, the rocky places, and the thorns are *not* part of our lives. If we have rid ourselves of those things, then the spots where they were now stand empty—empty and, once again, full of potential for good growth.

FULL FROM EMPTY

At the scene of Christ's first miracle, when He changed water to wine, He said very little. Notice He didn't pass a hand over the water, look at it, or even inspect it before it was taken to the master of the banquet. Instead, He knew the jars were empty, He told the servants to fill them, and then He knew the abundant simple water had been changed to a high quality commodity. Hmmm. Sounds a bit like Christ himself. He was a simple man, the son of a carpenter. But after this first miracle, His glory was revealed. From the starting point of empty containers came the fullness of just who this Man was.

Who were the first people affected by this miracle? The servants. Not the master, not the bride and groom, not the more honored guests, but the servants. Why is this important? Because it is the humble who will find themselves most affected by Christ.

The same is true for us. It is the humble who live a surrendered life to their Master. It is the humble who have little to offer but honest service. It is the humble who are free from obstacles that would otherwise prevent the Word from being sown well and deep in their lives. It is the humble whom the Lord most wants as His sowers and reapers.

> IT IS THE HUMBLE WHO LIVE A SURRENDERED LIFE TO THEIR MASTER.

THE HEARTBREAK OF SURRENDER

One of my horses has a strong "fight or flight" instinct, meaning if he senses anything dangerous he leaps or takes off at a gallop before waiting to see what is so frightening. He runs first and asks questions later.

In the wild an animal will flee when threatened, but fight if cornered. Teeth and hooves and horns all make for a nasty, bloody defense system. Whether running away in fear or fighting for their lives, surrendering is not an option. Death is the price of defeat.

It also is against our nature as humans to surrender. Our instinct is to fight hard for what we want or need. If we can't fight, we run (think about where this got Jonah). Yet these very qualities that God created in us turn against us and act as obstacles when He wants us to surrender. We hold on tight like a child gripping a piece of candy, absolutely certain if we let go very bad things will happen. But He needs us to surrender for better things to come.

I've held many hopes and dreams in my life. Some were born of selfish ambition, others of truly wanting God's best. Still others I'm waiting on, hopeful the Lord will bring them to pass. I've had to learn to surrender my wants and hopes simply because they are "mine." I've had to learn if I truly want God's best, because I know it is *the best*, I can't act independently. When I've surrendered my wants, the "in" of independence drops and I'm left with dependence. All things considered, I'd rather be dependent on Him than independent or dependent on me. I'm not reliable. I know He is.

How can we surrender when it feels so hard? Imagine standing before a giant medieval oak door. The keys are hanging right in the lock. The only problem is your hands are full of *you*: your wants, desires, wishes, and dreams. Then there's a voice from the other side of the door: "Come to me." More than anything you want to be on the other side of that giant door, because you know in Christ's presence you will find a satisfying love-relationship with Him, full of peace, blessing, and safety. But your arms and hands are so laden that you can't turn the key in the lock or open the door. All your wants are keeping you locked out from God's presence. What's the solution? Everything has to be dropped. Your arms have to let go, letting it all fall to the floor in surrender. When it all drops in a giant heap and you step over it to turn the key and open the door, you'll find the Lord waiting for you. The problem is, the stuff is still sitting there. What will the Lord ask you to do with it? Get rid of it. Just because you've surrendered doesn't mean it's disappeared. Now it's time to let it go as a complete sacrifice.

THE SACRIFICE OF SELF

No one wants to hear about the need for sacrifice in one's life. We interpret sacrifice as losing something: loss of identity, wants, needs, home, or even life itself. Remember, God doesn't demand sacrifice for the sake of demanding. He doesn't want our offerings of sacrifice to feel like loss. Sacrifice must be freely made from a heart that is pure and desirous of God and His will alone.

"God loves a cheerful giver" (2 Corinthians 9:7). Webster's says cheerful means "joyful, bright, attractive, willing, and ready." We mistakenly think this verse about giving cheerfully is just about giving money or tithing to our churches. But the Lord wants us to cheerfully give ourselves to Him. All other sacrifice follows that.

> WHATEVER HE IS ASKING US TO SURRENDER IN SACRIFICE NEEDS TO BE MOVED OUT OF THE WAY FOR HIS BEST TO COME ABOUT.

God's sought-after cheerfulness in our hearts isn't from the work He has asked us to do or the sacrifice He's asking us to make. A cheerful or happy heart comes from knowing absolutely that the Lord would never ask us to sacrifice something if He didn't have something even better to give us in its place. God isn't a taker. He's a giver. Whatever He is asking us to surrender in sacrifice needs to be moved out of the way for His best to come about.

That surrender may be of our own ambitions. We have plans, expectations, and agendas about where we feel our lives are going. These may be great and noble ideas. But if we haven't submitted them to God, and they aren't mapped out by His hand, they aren't His *best* for us. What we think is right sometimes is not God's way, because He says His thoughts and ways are not our thoughts and ways (See Isaiah 55:8–9). His thoughts and plans are higher, bigger, and broader, with a far-reaching, high-impacting intent. In other words, we think too small! We need to sacrifice what we think is *good* to make way for God's *best*.

> WE CAN'T OFFER A SACRIFICE IF WE SACRIFICE NOTHING FOR THE OFFERING.

We can't offer a sacrifice if we sacrifice nothing for the offering. In the Old Testament the sacrifice offerings were always the *best* people had to offer: the first harvest yield, the unblemished lambs, the new wine. But what was He always after from these sacrifice offerings? The people's hearts. Their hearts had to be full of trust—that there would be more crops to harvest and more young lambs to be born—and obedience.

Psalm 51:17 reminds us, "The sacrifices of God are a broken spirit; a broken and contrite heart, O God, you will not despise." What is a broken and contrite heart? A teachable heart. This is not the same as being downhearted, which is a feeling of discouragement. You can have a broken heart for God with a big smile on your face. Brokenheartedness for the Lord is having a thirst for His intent in your life and for His big world. A contrite heart is a heart that is willing to be molded for God's purposes. Oswald Chambers said, "If through a broken heart God can bring His purposes to pass in the world, then thank Him for breaking your heart" (*My Utmost for His Highest,* November 1 reading).

Someone once said it's hard to offer a living sacrifice if it keeps trying to crawl off the altar. Which is exactly what we do. We say we surrender, we say we are willing to be a living sacrifice, but we keep trying to get out of it. We have to learn to have the staying power, the will not to live but to die to ourselves.

Paul wrote to the Roman church, "Therefore, I urge you, brothers, in view of God's mercy, to offer your bodies as living sacrifices, holy and pleasing to God—this is your spiritual act of worship" (Romans 12:1). He is saying when we consider the mercy of God that nailed His only Son to the cross, the least we can do, the smallest sacrifice we can make in return, is to offer our entire beings back to Him. This is a thank-offering sacrifice. Each and every day we need to offer ourselves as living, willing, cheerful sacrifices for God's service.

THE BEST, FIRST, AND LAST

An emptying of ourselves is what leads us to be able to give freely. Jesus said the greatest commandment of all the laws and prophets is to love Him with all of our heart, soul, mind, and strength (Mark 12:29–31). All of us, for all of Him. The Lord doesn't want our leftovers: not of our time, money, or hearts. He wants the best of us from the start.

Why does God the Father ask for our best first? Because this is what He's given us in Christ. This is what He has modeled to us as our Abba Father. God gave us His best and only Son, first and last. He says He is the Alpha and the Omega, the beginning and the end. He gave us His first and only as the last-ever-needed sacrifice.

When the master of the wedding banquet unknowingly tasted the miraculous wine, he said to the bridegroom, "Everyone brings out the choice wine first and then the cheaper wine after the guests have had too much to drink; but you have saved the best till now" (John 2:10). This wedding banquet was unique because not only did the servants serve excellent wine at the beginning, they served even better wine at the end. This is a divine parallel to God the Father saving the best, His only Son, as the last sacrifice.

This wedding also marked the beginning of the end for Christ. The banquet, to which He had been invited because His mother was a guest, served as the turning point in His ministry. It's not coincidental Jesus' first miracle took place at a wedding. I believe there is a multidimensional meaning behind this life-changing miracle. To me, the banquet symbolizes Christ coming together with His bride: the church. He had come to the banquet as a man, but in the transformation of water to wine, He showed himself as the Bridegroom of God's church. He was now fully equipped to minister, and He was empty of anything but His Father's plans. He was fully prepared also to empty himself in complete sacrifice of His time and energies to bring fullness into the empty laws and regulations of religious tradition.

His ministry was to give spiritual drink to the thirsty. It was to give depth and meaning to the Law of Moses. It was to fill the empty places in the lives of people who ached for more than tradition. It was for people who wanted to be changed from everyday "water" to high quality "wine."

His ministry hasn't changed. We are what changes. Like the

empty vessels standing ready to be filled, are you ready to be filled by His Word and then transformed into the best He has for you?

Draw Near to Him:

What kind of vessel are you? Empty and ready to be filled and useful? Or are there "things" in your vessel that need to be sacrificed so you can have empty places for the Lord to continue His work in you? Remember, starting empty makes us full of potential.

Drink From His Cup:

"Therefore, I urge you, brothers, in view of God's mercy, to offer your bodies as living sacrifices, holy and pleasing to God—this is your spiritual act of worship. Do not conform any longer to the pattern of this world, but be transformed by the renewing of your mind" (Romans 12:1–2).

CHAPTER EIGHT

REFILLED VESSELS

My mare's newborn foal, a strapping colt, stood wobbly for the first time. His long legs stuck out from his body like oversized toothpicks. In a dazed, uncoordinated stumble-walk he headed straight for what his instincts told him he needed: his mother's udder. His little lips quivered and his tongue made a smacking noise as he tried to steady himself against her side for his first drink. After several minutes of trying to latch on to her leg, then her belly, then her quarters, he finally found what he was looking for. Warm, sweet milk dripped out of the sides of his mouth. In a short time he simply crumpled into a neat pile on the straw and quickly dozed off, sated but exhausted from his first meal. Full of the goodness of his mother's milk, he slept peacefully as his mother stood guard over him.

I remember this tender scene from sixteen years ago and recall how I felt impressed by the thought that when we are filled with good things, things sweet to our souls and spirits, we can rest in peacefulness.

In the previous chapter we learned when we are empty we are full of potential. We can now learn about what good things the Lord wants to fill us with and invest in us.

When we thirst for the Lord and we desire to have our yearning quenched by Him alone, what do we think will satisfy that thirst? Only God, of course. He "satisfies [our] desires with good things" (Psalm 103:5). To have our thirst for Him satisfied we need to be full of the good things of Him: His character, His heart, and His wisdom. He *wants* to give us these good things.

Christ's character was reflected in the miracle of changing water to wine at the wedding banquet. In an act of show-and-tell, He took the empty jars and then, using the water that filled them, provided what was needed: fine wine.

> HE WANTS THE EMPTY PLACES
> OF OUR LIVES TO
> BE FILLED WITH THE
> GOOD THINGS OF HIM.

Similarly, He wants the empty places of our lives to be filled with the good things of Him.

THE INDWELLING SPIRIT

Before Jesus was even birthed into Mary's arms she had a sense of wonder and excitement and anticipation about what she had been chosen for. In Luke 1:46–55, Mary sings a song of praise and trust to the Lord in response to her pregnancy and her cousin Elizabeth's encouragement. Her song speaks of her own humility and how the Lord honors a humble heart above a proud heart. She remembers God's faithfulness to her ancestors and sees her legacy as a continuation of God's promises. Her global perspective was part of the reason God chose her. She may have had a deep understanding of the all-encompassing Lord she served, but she remained singularly humble.

At one point in her heartfelt song her words reflect the psalmist's: "He has filled the hungry with good things" (Luke 1:53). Who are the hungry she speaks of, and, once again, what are the "good things"?

This speaks of her own hunger for the things of God. After her initial question about her virgin status when the angel Gabriel first appeared to her, head bowed in humility, she says, "I am the Lord's servant. . . . May it be to me as you have said" (Luke 1:38). She wanted to fulfill God's call on her life; she was hungry for it, regardless of what it might cost her personally. She knew a humble heart would ask for a thirst-quenching drink; a proud heart won't.

Like Mary, we can have the Holy Spirit come upon us and the power of the Most High overshadow us to become full of the good things of God (v. 35). Our prayer can be, "Make me pregnant with your indwelling Spirit."

When I was pregnant with my second child, my belly popped out fast. It didn't help that I gained too much weight. It was noticeable from the start I was expecting, and people frequently took the liberty to ask all the typical questions of when I was due, if I knew whether I was having a boy or a girl, etc.

But the experience of what felt like a very "public" pregnancy gave me a sense of how I want the indwelling Holy Spirit to be evident in my life. I want it to be obvious—so much so that people ask me about it. I want the Spirit of the Living God to grow in me so complete strangers feel at liberty to ask me questions.

Galatians 4:6 says, "God sent the Spirit of his Son into our hearts." This Spirit provides the potential for growing good things in our souls. God's indwelling Spirit fills us with Christ-likeness, which overflows into our daily lives.

Ephesians says to "be filled with the Spirit" (5:18). And Galatians reminds us, "Since we live by the Spirit, let us keep in step with the Spirit" (5:25). Interpretation: the Spirit of the Living God is the "good" in us. The Spirit's influence then directs where we set our feet and hands.

When the Holy Spirit inhabits our souls and lives we become the house of God. A working, living, breathing building that has God's kingdom established in it. Second Corinthians 6:16 confirms this, saying our bodies are the temple

> WHEN THE HOLY SPIRIT INHABITS OUR SOULS AND LIVES WE BECOME THE HOUSE OF GOD.

of the Living God. Temples are places of honor and respect. They are filled with good things: valuable, golden, and beautiful.

RARE AND BEAUTIFUL TREASURES

We sometimes assume "good things" are material possessions, and yes, those may be by-products of God's good blessings. But the true treasure is coming to know God in a deeper love-relationship. Because when we know Him better our thirst for Him is closer to being quenched.

Proverbs 24:3–4 gives us this image: "By wisdom a house is built, and through understanding it is established; through knowledge its rooms are filled with rare and beautiful treasures." The Lord wants the rooms of our hearts to be filled to overflowing with the beauty of who He is and His glory. Nothing else is as beautiful or as valuable. These are indeed "good things."

King David, a man of wealth, power, handsome good looks,

a strong leader, and a warrior, said these words: "You are my Lord; apart from you I have no good thing" (Psalm 16:2). David knew he was nothing. His good traits, power, wealth, and leadership qualities amounted to nothing without God.

As David said, if we are separated from God we are separated from good things. Not only God's good blessings in our lives but also the goodness of God himself. God's generosity is unlimited; it is part of His very character.

So often we overlook the good things of God or miss them completely. We don't recognize His blessings because we aren't looking for them in the right places. His blessings don't necessarily reside in the width of our wallets. They aren't rooted in the materialism of what we own. They are built on the unseen, yet knowable, foundation of God's Word.

SEEK AND FIND

The Lord's very first blessing to us is His Word. Psalm 119:18 says, "Open my eyes that I may see wonderful things in your law." God's Word—His Law—is a treasure chest of "wonderful things." Like gold nuggets, the value of understanding His Word is the greatest blessing known to mankind.

The gospel of John begins, "In the beginning was the Word, and the Word was with God and the Word was God." Then, "The Word became flesh" (1:1, 14). Simply put, the Word of God that we hold in the form of our Bibles came in the flesh as Christ. Makes me not want to let it collect dust. How about you?

All other blessings in our lives flow from this source. Knowing the Word in person through a one-on-one love-relationship with Christ gives us new vision, new understanding, new insight.

As a friend of mine said after she had surgery on her eyes to correct farsightedness, "I didn't know what I couldn't see." We don't know what we can't see if we aren't looking for the blessings of God found in His Word. He calls His Word bread. We are starving ourselves—albeit unintentionally and unknowingly, but hungry just the same—when we don't ingest God's Word.

GOD REVEALED

I regularly pray for God to reveal himself to me. I want to know His heart; I want to feel what He feels. I've also learned to brace myself for when God answers this prayer. Because when He does show me His heart, it sometimes hurts.

One day my husband and I were driving home from an outing with our children. We listened to a worship CD as we discussed ideas about installing a new kitchen. As Peter talked about the benefits of a granite countertop, the words of a song on the CD pierced me: "O Lord, restore the church that bears your name. . . ." I started sobbing. As Peter droned on about countertop colors and costs, oblivious to my tears, I could feel the anguish that God feels about the brokenness of His church—His bride. My heart hurt—not a physical pain, but a broken and sad heart at the cost to relationships, brotherhood, and unity because we don't understand the price He paid for the "Word to become flesh." I could sense all He wants is to see us filled with joy and love and peace for one another, but His church—you and I equal culprits—have trampled the investment of His Son on earth.

This was a hard revelation, one that stung, but a blessing all the same. How could such heart pain be a *blessing*? Because I saw God's heart. Because I felt God's pain. Because He gave me what I asked for. He counted me as a worthy emissary for a revelation. I could not help but feel blessed despite the pain.

THE BLESSINGS OF
HARD REVELATIONS

Elisha knew the pain of a hard revelation. Second Kings 8 tells the story of a sick king, a greedy servant, and a great man of God. These players reveal the most base and the best of God's created humanity.

Ben-Hadad, king of Aram, is sick. And scared. He fears his illness will cause his death. But on hearing that Elisha, a well-known, godly man, is in town, the king sends his trusted servant, Hazael, to ask Elisha if King Ben-Hadad is going to die. This is how the story unfolds:

> Elisha answered, "Go and say to him, 'You will certainly recover'; but the Lord has revealed to me that he will in fact die." He stared at him with a fixed gaze until Hazael felt ashamed. Then the man of God began to weep.
>
> "Why is my lord weeping?" asked Hazael.
>
> "Because I know the harm you will do to the Israelites," he answered. (10–12)

Elisha then goes on to prophesy to Hazael just how murderously vile he would become when greed for the throne grabbed his heart. Not twenty-four hours later King Ben-Hadad suffocates at the hands of Hazael. But hadn't Elisha said the king would not die from the illness? Yes, he had. Elisha knew God's perfect plan was that the king would survive his ailment, but God had revealed to Elisha the murderous heart of Hazael: though the king should have survived his illness, he would not survive his greedy servant.

It's Elisha's response through this that so intrigues me. He wept. He sobbed. Not because he knew the king's life would be taken, but he cried and mourned for the nation of Israel. It felt bitter and it hurt and there was little he could do to change the revelation God gave him. God's chosen people would suffer severely at the hands of Hazael. This was the blessing of a hard revelation for Elisha.

Blessing?! How could the foreknowledge of such devastation be a blessing? Because when God reveals something to us we are co-joined with Him. We are not at arm's length but have been granted entrance into the "Holy of Holies." It's here we can be most useful to the Lord. It's here that our prayer of "Lord, establish your kingdom in me" has been answered. Just as Elisha saw into Hazael's heart, we can see into the heart of God's intent. We catch a glimpse of the giant canvas on which God works. If we thirst for God to reveal himself to us we'd better not be afraid or complain when He does! The blessing is that when He does answer our prayer to know His heart, we know He has *heard* our prayer!

HIDDEN BLESSINGS?

When we ask the Lord to reveal himself or a situation to us, we ask as if it's hidden somewhere. I don't believe God hides His plan from us. I think we look in

> WE NEED TO BE REVEALED TO HIS PLAN, NOT IT TO US.

the wrong places and assume it's hidden. We need to be revealed to His plan, not it to us. We need to learn to pray for eyes to see and ears to hear and feet to walk in the right direction. There's no hidden mystery to the fact that through the indwelling Holy Spirit the Lord is always communicating to us. The problem is our viewfinder for the blessings and good things of God is too small.

Let me give you an example. My family lives one-and-a-half miles from the base of a four-thousand-foot mountain. The mountain is obvious; we can't miss it looking out our windows. But with the naked eye we can't see what's going on near the summit. We know people pilgrimage to the top of the mountain on clear days; we've done it ourselves. Knowing they are there but not being able to see them left us wanting to see *more*. So Peter bought us a telescope for Christmas one year. Through the telescopic lens we can now eye little stick figures climbing across the granite top, see individual trees, and make out the nuances of the cliff faces.

The people weren't *hidden* from us; we just needed the right instrument to be able to see them. So too are God's revelations. They aren't hidden from us; we just need the right tools to be able to see them.

BLESSINGS FROM BAD CHOICES

Because we can see the bigger picture, even if it's a hard revelation of hurt and pain, we can have confidence that in the viewfinder of God's telescopic lens we will see that "all things [will] work together for good" (Romans 8:28 KJV).

But let's not confuse "all things work[ing] together for good" as a hall pass to cheap grace. This doesn't mean we can deliberately do something wrong, thinking God will blithely weave it into the tapestry of His good plan. Our side trips will have consequences. Our mistakes will delay the intended original blessing of God—if only we had followed the right directions.

I remember as a child trying to knit a little sweater for one of my dolls. My grandmother, an avid knitter—the kind who could carry on a conversation, drink tea, and knit a fancy-patterned sweater all at once—had taught me the basic knitting knots. But the sweater for my little doll had lumps and twists and knots all in the wrong places. I went to my grandmother in tears. She gently took my knitting needles, pulled them out from the carrying loops of yarn, and *ripped back at least five lines of knitting!* I cried harder. She said, "Sometimes you have to rip out the bad knots to make it right."

This was a soul lesson too. God will gently but firmly peel back the bad so something good can be created in its place.

There is great hope in the statement that all things will work together for good to those who love God. Hope because we don't have to rely on ourselves for the good to come. We don't have to wring our hands and say, "I hope it all works out." We can *know* it will work out when we leave our errors in God's hands. Even a situation we have totally messed up God will work for good. He will bring "good things" from bad choices if our hearts are repentant and teachable to a new way of operating or a new attitude.

> HE WILL BRING "GOOD THINGS" FROM BAD CHOICES IF OUR HEARTS ARE REPENTANT AND TEACHABLE.

THE BLESSING OF PEACE

This is the blessing of peace: a bad situation that only by God's tender hands unfolds into a form of rebirth. The amazing thing is we can live daily in this kind of peace. We feel it most profoundly when we've found ourselves on the far side of a crisis. But daily peace is affordable without the cost of a bad situation.

Psalm 119:165 offers this hope: "Great peace have they who love your law, and nothing can make them stumble." So how do we keep our footsteps steady? Start by *loving* God's law. That's His Word. We can't know the blessing of peace and live by peace if we don't know from where that peace is born. We can't daily trust in God's amazing peace if His Word isn't treasured with love in our hearts.

Colossians 3:15 reminds us by what we are to be daily governed. "Let the peace of Christ rule in your hearts, since as members of one body you were called to peace." If Christ's peace is ruling our hearts, and our actions are born of what's in our hearts, then peace should dictate our external lives.

IF PEACE RULES, THEN WE WILL BE AT PEACE!

If we are "ruled" by something it means we are under its influence, we are governed by it, it dictates our thoughts and actions. We can choose to be ruled by many things: food, other people, political ideals, even religiosity. But this verse tells us to "let" peace rule our lives. In other words, we have to allow the peace of Christ a place in our hearts to be able to have our lives under its influence. And do you know what the result is? If peace rules, then we will be at peace! Like an electrical conductor, peace carries what is inside—Christ—to shine on the outside of us.

EXTERNAL BLESSINGS

We will have eyes to see external blessings only if we are living in God's internal blessings. This is why the Lord always starts with our interiors when He talks about any changes in our lives.

As rivers of clear water wind their way to ever-bigger bodies of water and eventually to the ocean, so too do the internal blessings of God wind their way through our spirits until they flow naturally out of our lives.

The psalmist said, "I lift up my eyes to the hills—where does my help come from?" (Psalm 121:1). We need to lift up our eyes, lift up our countenance, lift up our thoughts to a higher, more holy place than ourselves. From this view we'll see God. It's through this telescopic lens we'll make out details of the blessings. We are so accustomed to scanning the horizon of our lives for possible threats that we forget to let our gaze linger on the good things right in front of us across the landscape.

In the past I have been terrified of my son getting sick. Any "normal" childhood virus, which for other children is quickly recoverable, can for my son last for days of scary out-of-control diabetes management. I spent the entire first winter after his diagnosis of diabetes dreading every school day, living from doom to doom. But after three years this got tiring, because most of the time he was really quite healthy. In my state of impending doom I had completely missed his far more frequent healthy days. When I realized my fear of his getting sick had robbed me of many good days, I got mad. At myself. Why hadn't it occurred to me to be grateful for all the healthy days?

I've learned to thank the Lord every day for a day of health. They are a blessing, and as soon as I realized this, I found the gloom and fear dissipated.

When Jordan was ten and just entering fifth grade, one day I heard him singing, "This is the day that the Lord has made, let us rejoice and be glad in it!" I believe he has been witness to my seeing each day as a blessing, always certain of the silver lining, and he too is rejoicing in each day's gift. The day—in and of itself—is a blessing. Each day is a unique—like-none-other—day created by God for His purposes, for us to live in and enjoy to the fullest.

> BLESSINGS HAVE A WAY OF MULTIPLYING WHEN WE SAY THANK-YOU EVEN FOR WHAT OTHERS MIGHT CONSIDER MUNDANE.

What blessings will you look for each day, acknowledge before God, and then accept with thanksgiving? Maybe a lovely home, maybe a special friend, maybe a car that started the first time in winter! Be sure to thank the Lord daily for these "small" external blessings.

Blessings have a way of multiplying when we say thank you even for what others might consider mundane.

"Seven times a day I praise you for your righteous laws," the psalmist says (119:164). Because God's law—His handbook for how we can live our daily lives in peace, joy, and freedom—is our greatest blessing, we have every reason to want to praise Him seven times a day. I took this verse literally and started intentionally praising God seven times a day. I praised Him when I first woke up—whether it was a beautiful day outside or gray and rainy. I praised Him for my family—whether they were irritating me that day or not. I praised Him for my work, even if I was too distracted by phone calls to really get anything done. I simply praised Him—whether or not it "felt" like anything to praise Him for. Guess what happened? My eyes began to see, really see, the blessings all around me that I had overlooked or taken for granted. My overall countenance lightened and peace and joy felt like constants in my heart.

If you have lived on the cusp of doom for years, you may be empty of any sort of praise and thankfulness. All thoughts are turned inward to the gnawing emptiness.

The Lord wants to fill those empty, joyless places with peace and new vision to see His hand at work. Just as He changed the humdrum of plain water to excellent wine, He wants to change you from looking inward to seeing Him in a new way through His character of goodness. Drink deep of His abundant good blessings. There will always be a ready supply, and it will bring a quenching of your thirst for Him.

Draw Near to Him:

Do you want the empty places in your life to be filled with the indwelling Holy Spirit? Pray for the Spirit to come in and take up residence in your life.

What are the "good things" in your life for which you can daily thank God? Pray for the Lord to open your eyes to His goodness all around you.

Drink From His Cup:

"I lift up my eyes to you, to you whose throne is in heaven. . . . [O]ur eyes look to the Lord our God, till he shows us his mercy" (Psalm 123:1–2).

CHAPTER NINE

USEFUL VESSELS

I boarded a small twin-engine plane bound for Chicago from Little Rock, Arkansas, on the first leg of a journey home to New Hampshire. I had been visiting FamilyLife Today in Little Rock to do an interview with Dennis Rainey about one of my books. I walked onto the plane with a light step and a smile. After a good taping session with Dennis and his sidekick, Bob Lepine, I was feeling pretty good. No, actually I was feeling pretty smug. I had *arrived*. I had shaken Dennis Rainey's hand and sat across from him in a recording studio, and I was most certainly *somebody*!

As the plane lifted off I settled into my seat next to the window with a fifty-something gentleman to my right. I pulled a book from my bag and started reading. About halfway through our flight, the man next to me started fidgeting. I moved closer to the window, trying to give him some space. Out of the corner of my eye I saw him pull out the little white bag from the seat pocket in front of him. Uh-oh. I knew I was in trouble. Sure enough, in a minute he was retching into the bag. Even though I have a degree in nursing, I have never been comfortable with sickness, especially not thirty thousand feet in the air. I felt a twinge of panic—I wanted *away* from this guy and his sickness. In a few brief minutes I went from feeling pretty special to feeling pretty miserable. Then God touched my heart and I felt the Spirit say to me: "Take care of my people. If you can't care for my people, it doesn't matter whose hand you've shaken; it doesn't matter who has read your books. What matters is *people.*"

Taking a deep breath (through my mouth), I turned to the man and patted his back as he again retched. Over the next half hour I handed him tissues, offered him a stick of gum, and tried to talk to him to get his mind off of his stomach. It didn't really work—by the time we landed he looked horrible. As we rolled to the gate I pressed the flight attendant call button, and they escorted him off the plane first. The last time I saw him he was tottering to the terminal, white bag in hand.

Okay, so this was pretty disgusting, but sometimes the Lord has to use uncomfortable situations in our lives to make a point.

As God's chosen people we are chosen to respond as Christ did: with love. Christ didn't turn away in disgust from the lepers who called to him from a distance. Christ didn't turn away from the woman with a bleeding disorder. He responded with true love. "Love is patient, love is kind. It does not envy, it does not boast, it is not proud. It is not rude, it is not self-seeking." This may be what my mind tells me, but taking action on it is drowned out by the annoyingly loud "resounding gong and clanging cymbal" in my heart

> PRIDE INDEED GOES BEFORE A FALL IF LOVE ISN'T THE PLATFORM ON WHICH WE STAND.

(1 Corinthians 13:4–5, 1). Pride indeed goes before a fall if love isn't the platform on which we stand.

USEFUL TO MANY

When Jesus changed the water to wine in the clay vessels, it was changed so it would be useful to many. It wasn't changed for the exclusive enjoyment of just one person. If it were intended only for the master of the banquet, Jesus would have changed only one goblet full. Instead, He counted everyone there worthy of receiving His miracle. His miracles were never exclusive. Frequently taking place in a crowd, in front of many, one act could change multiple lives at a time. What a ripple effect.

That is the basic ministry of Christ, and through us it is to be shared. At the beginning of this book we looked at how we all thirst for the things of God; it is a universal condition. We do not thirst alone. When we have known thirst and then found a fulfilling measure, we have a responsibility to share it with others. "So that there should be no division in the body, but that its parts should have equal concern for each other" (1 Corinthians 12:25).

That's what the filled vessels of wine were: they were useful to others. If we too are filled with the good things of God, as we discussed in the previous chapter, then we are useful to others too.

CHRIST IN ME SHOULD BRING OUT THE BEST IN ME.

My human response to the sick man on the plane was revulsion. But because Christ is in me—as new wine, the *best* wine offering, I could respond with

Christ's love and goodness. Christ in me should bring out the best in me. Christ in you should bring out the best in you too.

It was Christ's power that changed the water to wine. It is this same power *in us* that can change a situation from something useless to something useful. "Therefore, as we have opportunity, let us do good to all people" (Galatians 6:10). Notice it doesn't give us the out of a caveat: "As long as they aren't doing something really gross."

BALANCED SCALES

The words *as we have opportunity* are a clue to recognizing seasons of possibility. Sometimes we fail to recognize the right action for the right season. In our zeal, or lack of zeal, we miss opportunities. But our zeal for recognizing opportunities needs to be balanced with discernment.

Discernment and wisdom stand hand in hand at the scales of a balanced life. Proverbs 2:10–11 tells us in what way wisdom will help to balance us: "For wisdom will enter your heart, and *knowledge* will be pleasant to your soul. *Discretion* will protect you and *understanding* will guard you" (emphasis added). This is a threefold promise. When our lives are governed by God's wisdom and discernment in a situation it protects us from getting out of balance. The *knowledge* of God's timing for a situation will comfort our souls and give us peace that the timing is in His hands and we don't need to jump

> DISCERNMENT AND WISDOM STAND HAND IN HAND AT THE SCALES OF A BALANCED LIFE.

on the crisis bandwagon of rescuing people. Knowing our season is having the *discretion* to know when to speak and when to be silent.

Just because God gives us a free will doesn't mean we have the freedom to bring harm to His kingdom. We need to avail ourselves of all three of the above-mentioned attributes to be sure we correctly handle opportunities.

The last phrase of the now-famous Jabez prayer says, "that I may not cause pain" (1 Chronicles 4:10 NKJV). To me, this is the most heartfelt part of this life-changing prayer. I don't want anything I say or do or think or act to cause pain to God's kingdom. I would rather He close my mouth for the remainder of my life than allow it to cause pain to Him, His kingdom, or His plans for His people.

WEIGHTED HEARTS

"Honest scales and balances are from the Lord; all the weights in the bag are of his making" (Proverbs 16:11). At face value this Scripture is about honesty and not cheating. No argument there. But it's also about balance—with balance is honesty. Hmmm. Does this mean if we are out of balance—even as noble as our intended actions may be—that we are being *dishonest*? I believe it does. It means we are being dishonest if we've put more weight in one area of our lives than another.

Take for example—a true story here—the man who completely neglected to support his family financially because he went out street-evangelizing every day. His family had no food, his children wore rags, but he daily pounded the pavement, not for a job but for souls. That's dishonesty. Dishonest, because he was not honest to the family responsibility God had given him.

The second part of the above verse is equally challenging: "All the weights in the bag." All the things that weigh us down, all the burdens God has placed on our hearts, are part of the divine mixture in God's hands. He is fully aware of the burdens He has put on our hearts. I've always had a burden for women facing unexpected pregnancies. I've also always felt heart pain for women who suffer from self-condemnation. But if I neglected all my other responsibilities in my life to "minister" to these kinds of women, the "weights in my bag" would put an undue burden on my family.

He invests "weights" in us but sometimes we have to *wait* to act on those burdens. We aren't born into salvation all grown up. It takes maturity—time—to wait for the right seasons to act on the burden He puts in us. But when the scales are balanced with perspective, and we read the season right, then we will be part of a bountiful kingdom harvest.

> IT TAKES MATURITY—TIME— TO WAIT FOR THE RIGHT SEASONS TO ACT ON THE BURDEN HE PUTS IN US.

LET'S LET THEM

One of the greatest mistakes we can make as Christians is to assume other people hold the same level of fire and passion for a cause as we do. God invests in each of us *different* things about which we will feel passionate. Mine is different than yours; yours will be different than the people sitting near you in church. All of God's causes are good and noble; it's just that we aren't all called to all of them.

With this in mind, some light is shed on Romans 12:4–8:

> Just as each of us has one body with many members, and
> these members do not all have the same function, so in
> Christ we who are many form one body, and each member
> belongs to all the others. We have different gifts, according
> to the grace given us. If a man's gift is prophesying, let him
> use it in proportion to his faith. If it is serving, let him serve;
> if it is teaching, let him teach; if it is encouraging, let him
> encourage; if it is contributing to the needs of others, let him
> give generously; if it is leadership, let him govern diligently;
> if it is showing mercy, let him do it cheerfully.

There's a key here to the basic ministry of one to another in
the church: *Let them.* In other words, we are to encourage others
to go ahead and use their gifts appropriately. There's freedom in
the words *let them.* Freedom for the person gifted in a particular
area to go and do, but equally as much, freedom for the person
not gifted in that area not to be forced to serve in a way in which
he or she isn't equipped.

AS USEFUL VESSELS WHO ARE HANDLING THE WORD OF TRUTH CORRECTLY, OUR ROLE IS TO EDIFY OTHERS.

The point of our
unique gifting is to edify
other people: to encourage
and build up. Galatians
6:4–5 reminds us, "Each
one should test his own
actions. Then he can take
pride in himself, without
comparing himself to
somebody else, for each one should carry his own load." What's
his "own load"? The burdens or "weights" of our hearts that God
has invested in us individually are our "load."

As useful vessels who are handling the Word of truth correctly, our role is to edify others. Since we don't thirst alone for the peace, grace, and blessings of God, our role is to help, encourage, and direct people to God by ministering through our gifts.

BALANCED WITH FRUIT

When I visit my doctor for an annual checkup, the first order of business is usually a closed-eye step onto the scale. I know what my scale at home says, but invariably the doctor's scale is about five pounds heavier. *Heavier!* So I go home depressed, step on my scale, and readjust its balance so it more or less matches the doctor's scale.

A scale is useless if it can't be balanced. This is true of the balanced scales we need in our Christian walk too. On one side God gives us a burden, a heavy heart for something, for somebody, or for a cause. The question is, what do we use to weight the other side to keep in balance? What do we have to keep our perspective in balance? Fruit. Not apples and oranges, but the fruit of the Spirit.

The singular fruit, made up of nine sections, is "Love, joy, peace, patience, kindness, goodness, faithfulness, gentleness and self-control" (Galatians 5:22–23). This fruit in our lives balances our heavy burdens so our burdens are put to good use. If our zeal for pre-born children is not tempered with self-control, for example, our burden is wasted because we may become out of control in our attempt to "save" babies. Or if our heart is weighted with a desire to teach, but we don't have patience for the various learning styles, we'll find ourselves frustrated. We have to function with the balance of the Spirit's fruit in our lives.

Where does this fruit come from? Galatians 5:22 begins, "The fruit of the Spirit . . ." In other words, the Holy Spirit of God, who indwells our hearts, does more than fill the empty places that were full of potential. The Spirit has a purpose. That purpose is to produce fruit. Godly fruit. This godly fruit is what makes our zeal for a cause productive. Otherwise it's only borne of us, and its potential reach is as limited as we are.

> THE FRUIT OF HIS SPIRIT
>
> IN US IS REFLECTED IN
>
> HOW WE LIVE OUR LIVES.

Have you ever considered that this fruit is of the Spirit, the very attributes of God himself? Our souls are inhabited by God's Spirit. The fruit of His Spirit in us is reflected in how we live our lives. As Ephesians 5:1 says, "Be imitators of God."

Let's think again about the transformation of the water into wine at the wedding banquet. What is wine made from? Fruit—usually grapes. Jesus wants to transform us in the same way: from empty vessels into vessels full of the fruit of the Spirit. The evidence of this fruit in our lives is the only thing that makes us useful.

Consider how each attribute of the Spirit's fruit defines God himself and how His Spirit in us will bear fruit in our lives.

LOVE

Love is listed first as part of the fruit of the Spirit because it is the most predominate attribute of God. He calls us to live in love that is like His. His perfect love is an example for us to live by. When we live *in* His love we are able to live *according* to His love. When we live according to His love, we respond to life's circumstances based on His limitless love and not on our limited resources.

First Corinthians 13, the well-known "love" chapter, ends with the words "And now these three remain: faith, hope and love. But the greatest of these is love." Why is love the greatest? Because

WHEN WE LIVE IN HIS LOVE

WE ARE ABLE TO LIVE

ACCORDING TO HIS LOVE.

love will always defeat evil. It did when Christ died, and it does when we are confronted with a hard circumstance. When the Spirit of God indwells us, love is the first manifestation of His fruit because it is the best attribute. It was God's best for us and it is the best way we can respond and act.

JOY

As the parent of a newborn child rejoices and marvels over the miracle of creation, so does our Lord marvel over each one of us—created in His image. Zephaniah 3:17 paints a vivid yet tender picture of just how precious we are to the Lord and how much joy He takes in who we are. "He will take great delight in you, he will quiet you with his love, he will rejoice over you with singing." Isn't that beautiful?

He is our Abba, "Daddy," Father, and He responds to us as a loving Father, with unconditional, full-acceptance adoration. He takes joy in our newfound baby steps when we've learned to stand on our own two feet. He takes joy in our newfound voice when we sing praises to Him. He takes joy when we cry out to Him in our dark times of confusion.

When His Spirit is dwelling in us, the joy He has for us is *in* us. This is sometimes hard to believe when circumstances seem to sweat the joy right out of you. Yet I've seen joy on the faces of the most afflicted people.

Not long after I graduated from nursing school I held a job at a community hospital. I worked on the medical-surgical floor, meaning my patients on any given day could be recovering from surgery, suffering a severe viral illness, dying of cancer, or "drying out" from an addiction.

One day I was assigned to a woman whom I vaguely knew from my family's church. She had cancer; she was in a coma. She had very few days left. I knew she knew the Lord, so every time I tended to her, I hummed hymns. She never woke from her coma, but she didn't have to. Her face communicated what was in her heart: the joy of God's presence in her. Whenever I hummed to her, her heartbeat quickened and her face held a steady, tranquil countenance. Though her circumstances were dire, her joy was palpable in her relationship with God. How was this possible?

The answer is in the love-relationship between the Vine and the branches. When Jesus talked about His role as the Vine and our role as the dependent branches in John 15, He talked about love as the connector of the relationship. But then He brought a whole new concept into the conversation. *Joy.* Joy is the nutrient carried through the Vine to the branches for a fuller, more bountiful, and glorious harvest. Jesus said, "I have told you this [to remain in God's love] so that my joy may be in you and that your joy may be complete" (v. 11). In other words, *Love is incomplete without joy.*

PEACE

Author and international speaker Joyce Meyer is fond of answering to difficult circumstances, "Keep your peace!" Her point is to keep our heads above the muddy waters of turmoil that threaten to overwhelm us. Hold on to peace! Don't let it go!

When we hold on to peace we are holding a piece of hope. I love the movie title *Hope Floats*. Hope rises to the surface, because hope always has the buoyancy of possibility. Peace and hope go hand in hand. Without hope we can't have the peace of knowing that all is truly, assuredly in the safety of God's hands.

> HOPE RISES TO THE SURFACE, BECAUSE HOPE ALWAYS HAS THE BUOYANCY OF POSSIBILITY.

When Paul told us to "live in" peace, he did so knowing that promoting peace would gird the foundation of the first two manifestations of the fruit of the Spirit: love and joy. Love and joy can't thrive in an unpeaceful environment.

PATIENCE

I am not, by nature, a very patient person. For years my husband and I talked about, made a dozen different plans for, and researched putting an addition onto our too-small-for-four-people-two-dogs-and-two-cats house. In Dorothy-like fashion, I wanted to click my heels, say a few words, and find myself in a new place. Now. The addition finally was built last summer.

I feel impatient with my children when they argue; I raise my voice at them, then feel impatient with myself for blowing the patient fruit to bits again. My impatience is self-perpetuating too. The more I spew impatience, the more the people around me are impatient.

I find it amazing and more than comforting to know that God doesn't get impatient the way we do. He may let us traverse the same ground over and over to let us learn a lesson, but that just proves how patient He is. He is long-suffering in our imperfections. Each human He creates is not a stab at a new and refined model; He's okay with our not being perfect. He is unfailingly patient with our imperfections.

> HE IS UNFAILINGLY PATIENT WITH OUR IMPERFECTIONS.

Patience means slow to anger. Notice it doesn't say is never angry. Just slow to anger. Have you ever taken a trip where you had two choices of how you could reach your destination: a quick trip along a speedy highway or a more meandering trip along back roads? Slow-to-anger in our relationships with others means we take the longer route to anger. And even if we arrive at a justifiable anger, we don't let it dictate or define our responses.

The fruit of patience in your life may take some tongue biting. But your patience, just as God's patience with you, nurtures rather than crushes other people's feelings.

KINDNESS

God's kindness to us shows in His concern for the smallest details of our lives, like a simple unexpected gift.

Why are random acts of human kindness random, and why are we so surprised by them? Because kindness is lacking in the world. We are a self-possessed, self-revolved, self-motivated culture. Sad to say, it takes a crisis to bring out kindness.

If kindness came naturally to us, various Proverbs and New

Testament references wouldn't need to carry instructions to be kind. "A kind man benefits himself" (Proverbs 11:17); "Whoever is kind to the needy honors God" (Proverbs 14:31); "Be kind and compassionate to one another" (Ephesians 4:32); "Always try to be kind to each other and to everyone else" (1 Thessalonians 5:15). We actually have to learn to be kind. Our survival-of-the-fittest nature doesn't usually let another go first in line.

Being kind is simply being *nice*. It means anticipating what someone might need without their asking. It means getting a drink of water for our spouse when we pour ourselves one. It means greeting our children after school with a pleasant smile and a few nice words. Being kind requires deliberate, thought-out acts.

> GOD'S KINDNESS TO US SHOWS IN HIS CONCERN FOR THE SMALLEST DETAILS OF OUR LIVES.

GOODNESS

"You are forgiving and good, O Lord, abounding in love to all who call to you" (Psalm 86:5). The New Testament is called the Good News because it is about God's awesome goodness through the news of Christ's birth, death, and resurrection.

But as with kindness, why do humans have to be instructed to "be good"? It seems so odd that what *should* come naturally we have to learn and practice. Paul reminds us several times in his letters to "do good" (see Galatians 6:9–10; Ephesians 2:10; and 1 Timothy 6:18). In our looking-out-for-my-own-needs culture, we have lost our sensitivity to other people and their needs.

Just as a severely burned hand can no longer feel sensations, we may be conditioned to no longer feel sensitivity toward other people's pain.

Goodness is not complex. It can be as simple as putting our trash in the right receptacle rather than out the car window. It's about being on time. It's about doing what you said you'd do. It's even about remembering relatives' and friends' birthdays.

I want to be able to stand before God and hear those words we all hope to hear when our days on earth have finished: "Well done, good and faithful servant!" (Matthew 25:21). This means that what we *do* is either good and faithful to God's intents or not good and unfaithful to God's intents. In carrying His Son's name—Christian—as part of who I am, I want goodness to be part of what God commends me for.

FAITHFULNESS

> IT'S A GOOD THING GOD'S LEVEL OF FAITHFULNESS TO US IS NOT DEPENDENT ON OUR LEVEL OF FAITHFULNESS TO HIM.

It's a good thing God's level of faithfulness to us is not dependent on our level of faithfulness to Him. Like the tide, our faithfulness can be fully in or far off. But His remains steady as the sun itself.

"Your kingdom is an everlasting kingdom, and your dominion endures through all generations. The Lord is faithful to all his promises and loving toward all he has made" (Psalm 145:13). He is a keep-on-keeping-on God. His faithfulness doesn't falter and never wavers.

A person who is faithful is one who is "standing firm" in God's strength and power. An example is Stephen, known as the first Christian martyr, who stood firm in faithfulness to the very end of his life (see Acts 6–7). He did not falter under the verbal and eventual stone-throwing attacks. The more his accusers rallied against him the more it fed his stubborn faith.

In the twenty-first century the stones may look different, but their target is the same: our hearts of faith. Our full armor of God (Ephesians 6) is what not only protects us from external threats but also

> GENTLENESS IS A QUIET DIGNITY THAT DOESN'T NEED TO RAISE ITS VOICE.

keeps our internal faith intact. When we are faithful and diligent in our relationship with God, our eyes will be more open to God's abiding faithfulness. Our faith is self-perpetuating from there. The more we stand in faith, the more we see God's hand upholding us.

GENTLENESS

All the times I've asked the Lord to show me an error in my ways or asked Him to reveal something to me, He's generally answered in a tender, gentle way. Some people need to be hit over the head, and I can be a blockhead too, but I believe God's preference is gentleness. He may resort to a heavier hand if gentleness doesn't get our attention, but like a quiet breeze before a storm, He'll start softly.

Gentleness is as gentleness does. That's why Proverbs 15:1 reminds us, "A gentle answer turns away wrath." When we respond to situations with a truly gentle voice and heart, it acts as a quieting influence.

Gentleness is a quiet dignity that doesn't need to raise its voice. "But in your hearts set apart Christ as Lord. Always be prepared to give an answer to everyone who asks you to give the reason for the hope that you have. But do this with gentleness and respect" (1 Peter 3:15). Notice it says to "be prepared," but it doesn't say, "Shout it out loud at every opportunity." Rather be ready with a soft answer when the opportunity presents itself.

SELF-CONTROL

When we really think about it, the Lord shows an awful lot of restraint. His promise to Noah in the rainbow, for example, is our assured inheritance displayed in the beauty of the colors and softness of the earthbound arc, speaking volumes of His divine self-control.

For us, out-of-control actions are borne from out-of-control thoughts. Our thoughts are like a runaway train once they catch hold of an idea, an image, or a plan. The brakes of restraint are thin, and we rush headlong into serious sin.

Paul talks about "[being] made new in the attitude of your minds" (Ephesians 4:23). He wouldn't have said this if we didn't need to watch the travel lines of our mind's attitudes. Self-control starts in the mind. Self-control for the Christian does not mean control of *self* so much as obedience to God's control through the "renewing of our minds" (Romans 12:2).

Interestingly, both of these verses refer to "new" minds. The old mind is one ruled by self; the new mind is one ruled by God. I picture self-control as the last manifestation of the Spirit listed because self-control acts like a zippered bag in which all the other manifestations of the fruit of the Spirit are kept. Self-control knows when to speak with goodness, kindness, and love, when to manifest patience, joy, peace, gentleness, and faithfulness. Self-control knows when to keep quiet if the words about to be spoken are less than good, loving, and kind.

POWER WALKING

First Corinthians 4:20 tells us, "The kingdom of God is not a matter of talk but of power." We can talk about the fruit of the Spirit all we want, but the true fruit is evident by the power it has in our lives. Are we walking and living in the power of spiritual fruit? Our usefulness as ambassadors and willing vessels for God's purposes is in direct proportion to the fruit of the Spirit in our lives.

> OUR USEFULNESS AS AMBASSADORS AND WILLING VESSELS FOR GOD'S PURPOSES IS IN DIRECT PROPORTION TO THE FRUIT OF THE SPIRIT IN OUR LIVES.

Our own vessels can be full to overflowing with the thirst-quenching good things of God and His new wine of the fruit of the Spirit. It's into these we can dip to offer a drink to others of God's family. Then they too can taste the thirst-quenching drink of God himself.

Draw Near to Him:

We all are vessels of importance to the Lord. None is too small; none is useless. Will you stand ready to be filled with His good things? What wine—or fruit—will pour forth from your vessel to nourish and encourage others? Will you learn to speak messages of hope, love, and faithfulness? Will your hands reach out with goodness, kindness, and patience?

Drink From His Cup:

"Live a life worthy of the calling you have received. Be completely humble and gentle; be patient, bearing with one another in love. Make every effort to keep the unity of the Spirit through the bond of peace" (Ephesians 4:1–3).

Part Four

LIVING ON THE WATER

JESUS WALKS ON THE WATER

Matthew 14:22–33

Immediately Jesus made the disciples get into the boat and go on ahead of him to the other side, while he dismissed the crowd. After he dismissed them, he went up on a mountainside by himself to pray. When evening came, he was there alone, but the boat was already a considerable distance from land, buffeted by the waves because the wind was against it.

During the fourth watch of the night Jesus went out to them, walking on the lake. When the disciples saw him walking on the lake, they were terrified. "It's a ghost," they said, and cried out in fear.

But Jesus immediately said to them: "Take courage! It is I. Don't be afraid."

"Lord, if it's you," Peter replied, "tell me to come to you on the water."

"Come," he said.

Then Peter got out of the boat and walked on the water and came toward Jesus. But when he saw the wind, he was afraid and, beginning to sink, cried out, "Lord, save me!"

Immediately Jesus reached out his hand and caught him. "You of little faith," he said, "why did you doubt?"

And when they climbed into the boat, the wind died down. Then those who were on the boat worshiped him, saying, "Truly you are the Son of God."

CHAPTER TEN

DARK TIMES

A s I sat in the cabin my husband built for me deep in the woods on our farm, I switched off the only source of light: a battery-operated lantern. Immediately the eight-by-ten-foot room fell into complete darkness. It was a clear night, but the canopy of heavily leaved trees outside the small windows hid the light of the stars. It was darker than dark. I couldn't even see my hand in front of my face. When I say the cabin "fell into darkness," that is exactly how it felt. Without light to see, I had the sensation of falling into something unknown, something confusing, something suddenly open without boundaries yet disturbingly pressing near.

I'm not afraid of the dark. But that night, my first alone in the cabin overnight, I felt frightened—not of the known bear, coyote, fox, deer, and moose outside my little cabin door but what was *inside*: inside of me.

My dark venture to the cabin was a deliberate attempt to "feel darkness." I've felt plenty of emotional darkness: the loss of my mother-in-law, whom I dearly loved, my son's chronic disease, a young friend's too-early death, the end of long-held dreams, shattered relationships, and even the passing of my pets; each has brought different levels of grief. Even still, I wanted to feel physical darkness.

Dark times, whether experienced privately or corporately, are marked by the same responses: feelings of vulnerable exposure and a deep desire for the light of understanding.

It took an amazing amount of self-discipline while I was in my cabin *not* to turn on the lantern. But always the choice was at my fingertips: I could reach out and push the switch on the lantern, and my senses would return to normal.

Far worse are the times when we have no choice but to weather the dark night while praying for an early dawn. Right before first light is when we think we can't bear the darkness any longer.

THE FOURTH WATCH

The first light comes during the fourth watch in the night, between 3 and 6 A.M. In the account of Jesus walking on the water, the fourth-watch watchman undoubtedly searched the horizon for the first light, a certain sign of encouragement, and perhaps even a change in the wind direction. The disciples were experiencing a "dark night" on three levels: a physical darkness, yes, but a spiritual and emotional darkness as well.

To understand what occupied the disciples' hearts and minds, let's look back to what happened only a few hours earlier. They had just ministered to, fed, and cleaned up after more than five thousand people sitting on a hillside. They must have felt exhausted. It had already been a long day; now the sun had set, and darkness had come, which was exactly what they had tried to avoid by asking Jesus to get moving *before* feeding the five thousand (Matthew 14:13–21). Even in their fatigue, Jesus *immediately* instructed them to get into their boat and start rowing. They rowed right into more darkness with dark water swirling under their hull, a fierce wind blowing against their oars, and since wind usually indicates stormy weather, likely a dark sky overhead.

Jesus deliberately sent His disciples into a dark place—a dark place where He was not present. It is suggested they felt abandoned and alone and frightened. Seeing what they thought was a ghost (which turned out to be Christ) only heightened their feelings of abandonment.

We've traversed those same waters. Though we know in our heads Christ will never abandon us, it sometimes feels in our hearts like He has. During dark times it feels as though He is indeed on a distant shore, off doing His own thing while He's cast us out into a very deep, very dark ocean of trouble.

Nothing will increase our thirst *more* for a cup of refreshing Living Water than feeling it has been withdrawn from our grasp. We need to realize this may be the very point of dark times. We've come far in this book about quenching our thirst for God and deepening our love-relationship with Him, but let me tell you a secret. He doesn't want our thirst ever to be fully quenched. He wants us always to be thirsting for more. Our thirst for Him will never be fully satisfied this side of heaven. He allows us to enter into dark times; He'll even

> HE ALLOWS US TO ENTER INTO DARK TIMES; HE'LL EVEN OCCASIONALLY LEAD US INTO DARK TIMES SO THAT OUR THIRST FOR HIM WILL INCREASE.

occasionally lead us into dark times so that our thirst for Him will *increase*.

THE SOURCE OF ALL COMFORT

Not many people live charmed lives. We all will suffer at some point. Suffering is what teaches us to draw on Christ and one another for comfort. Yes, ultimately Jesus is the source for our comfort and peace, but we are frequently the vessels that others may turn to first because we are present and tactile. People who haven't yet come into a personal love-relationship with Christ don't know He is what they are looking for. When they turn to Christians it's because they are seeing Christ and are drawn to the peace and perseverance they observe in a Christian's life.

> OUR DARK TIMES OF DOUBT OR FEAR OR CONFUSION ARE ACTUALLY NEEDED FOR US TO BE EFFECTIVE TOOLS FOR CHRIST.

Paul's second letter to the Corinthians starts with the admonition to comfort other people in the midst of their crisis. "The God of all comfort . . . comforts us in all our troubles, so that we can comfort those in any trouble with the comfort we ourselves have received" (1:3–4). In other words, our dark times of doubt or fear or confusion are actually *needed* for us to be effective tools for Christ.

When my son was diagnosed with type 1 diabetes, I didn't know any other families who had a child with the same disease.

I felt alone and scared. I felt as if Jesus had indeed put me on a boat and pushed me far offshore to manage the storm by myself. Then two things happened. First, an acquaintance sent me a note telling of her child's diagnosis just seven months before ours. Her words encouraged me and gave me hope that in time we wouldn't feel so overwhelmed and we could manage the disease. Around the same time, a friend commented that someday I might write about my son and our experience. I scoffed. I was still in the stage of spewing confusion and pain— no one would have wanted to read the words I would have written then.

Two years later I coauthored a book for families of children living with chronic medical conditions. I wouldn't have believed it myself, but the comfort I received from that encouraging note and connecting with other families who were raising "chronic kids" gave me the strength and witness to write words of comfort, hope, and wisdom. In full-life color it illuminated one of my favorite verses: "And we know that in all things God works for the good of those who love him, who have been called according to his purpose" (Romans 8:28).

Part of the "purpose" of our struggles is so God's goodness can be displayed. His goodness is the light of understanding we can bring to a situation. It's the flame of hope that we can ignite in other people.

A line from a song by Jerome Olds reminds us, "Don't forget in the darkness what we have learned in the light." When the sun sets in the West each day, do we forget what a bright sunny day looks and feels like? No. So why do we so quickly forget the experience of God's presence and the proof of His faithfulness when darkness shadows our faith? Because as the line from the above song says, we "forget" Christ's light when we are surrounded by spiritual darkness.

LIGHT OVERCOMES DARKNESS

"And God said, 'Let there be light,' and there was light. God saw that the light was good, and he separated the light from the darkness. God called the light 'day,' and the darkness he called 'night.' And there was evening and there was morning—the first day. . . . And God said, 'Let there be lights in the expanse of the sky to separate the day from the night.' . . . God made two great lights—the greater light to govern the day and the lesser light to govern the night" (Genesis 1:3–5, 14, 16).

I find these verses interesting because they communicate that from the beginning of time there was a *need* for light. Even though Adam and Eve hadn't yet been created and had therefore not yet sinned, the *potential* for evil was present from the start.

> LIGHT ALWAYS
> DISPERSES DARKNESS.

Why did God separate the light from the darkness? Because He saw the light was "good," and though it's not specifically stated, it's implied the darkness was "not good." They had to be separated because light and darkness cannot coexist. In one of God's greatest divine parallels between the life of nature and the nature of life, light always disperses darkness. They are diametrically opposed. You can't have both at the same time. That's why Christ called himself the Light of the World (John 8:12). The light of Christ always overcomes the darkness of everything that is not of Christ.

Being "in" the light of Christ prepares us to weather the dark of night. David penned the words "You are my lamp, O Lord; the Lord turns my darkness into light" (2 Samuel 22:29). In other words, the darkness in us—evil, sin, despair, wayward thoughts, pain, confusion—through God's divine intervention is turned into light: something good.

A "way" needs to be made for the light, however, and therein lies our responsibility. Let me give you a word picture.

Imagine a house being built. The foundation is poured, and the framing two-by-fours are erected for the walls. After constructing the roof, do the builders then cover all the interior walls with sheetrock and the exterior walls with siding? No, first they must frame in openings for windows. Of course, windows are made to let light in. No one would want a home that allowed no light to enter.

And so must a way be prepared and established to allow light to come into our lives. Building "windows" in our lives acknowledges that there will be times of darkness. This provides a way for the revelation of God's plan to enter our inner beings.

Let's take a look at the Proverbs 31 woman. She's not so annoyingly perfect as we sometimes think. There's a line that has held me captive for a number of years, telling us a lot about her inner spiritual walk. "Her lamp does not go out at night" (18). At first glance, this line seems to be about working hard, being diligent, and not being lazy. But there's a much deeper implication. "Night" is not just part of a twenty-four-hour day. There is also the threat of inner darkness. But the dark of night does not take her by surprise, nor does it overtake her. This is because she has anticipated darkness and has *prepared* for it. Her literal oil lamp does not go out because she has trimmed the wick and filled the vessel with fuel. But even more important, her *inner* lamp doesn't go out because she has filled her inner vessel with fuel too: the power of God's presence and an abiding love-relationship with Him. These are the windows for light to enter her soul.

The threatening circumstances in her life are probably not much different than what threatens our inner lives today. She was married to a businessman, she was raising a family, she worked outside of her home, she volunteered in her community, she cooked and cleaned and sewed and invited people to dinner. Sounds pretty familiar. But she knew these activities were a potential drain on all of her resources. She knew she could find herself in the darkness of fatigue, discouragement, and depression. She knew her personal spiritual reserves had to be full, just like her oil lamp, to face the dark night watches.

PREPARED LAMPS

The story of the ten virgins hits a nerve (see Matthew 25:1–13). Jesus is answering a question asked by His disciples about what the "end times" will look like. Jesus describes the decline of a civilized nation and how hate will lead to persecution of Christians. But, interestingly, He then talks about His church, the virgin bride, and His words take on a more personal tone. It's a message of how we as members of His church can be prepared for His appearance.

> NOT HAVING THE FUEL FOR LIGHT IS DENYING THE INEVITABILITY OF DARKNESS.

In the parable, half of the virgins took lamps with no oil. In twenty-first-century speak, that's like taking a flashlight on a camping trip—without batteries. Not having the fuel for light is denying the inevitability of darkness. These women, chattering and happy on their way to meet the bridegroom, completely ignored the simple fact of the setting sun. They faced the sunset with empty lamps.

On the other hand, the wise virgins had thought through

their trip and skipped on their way to meet the bridegroom, fully prepared with lamps full of oil and more in extra jars. It's a good thing, because the bridegroom took longer getting to them than was expected.

Interestingly, all ten women fell asleep during the night watch. In order to be able to fall asleep one has to be relaxed and confident in one's safety. The half with the extra oil were indeed safe in their preparations—they could relax and be confident, knowing even if they faced a night watch they were prepared with enough fuel in their lamps and extra in their jars. They rested in the secure arms of readiness.

But the other five slept in the cradle of ignorance. How and why did they fall asleep? Because they didn't know any better. They were foolish and hadn't been trained or instructed about why they would need extra oil. They lacked wisdom. They lacked practical knowledge. They lacked teaching even to know they needed to be prepared. Ignorance isn't bliss; it's dangerous and it's costly.

> IGNORANCE ISN'T BLISS; IT'S DANGEROUS AND IT'S COSTLY.

This is why so many Christians get into trouble in their faith walk. They don't know the basics of how to live the Christian life. One of the foundational tenants of our faith is to daily "work out your salvation . . . for it is God who works in you to will and to act according to his good purpose" (Philippians 2:12–13). This speaks of a responsibility we have in our love-relationship with God to allow Him to work in us to fulfill His purposes. This is what leading a godly life means; it's not about us, it's about Him in us. A godly life doesn't come about because we show up on Sunday for church. The five foolish virgins showed up at the wedding feast, but the Bridegroom (Christ) said, "I tell you the truth, I don't know you" (Matthew 25:12). Christ didn't know them because they had a lack of fuel, a lack of preparedness, a lack of recognition to be part of His kingdom.

> OUR ACTIONS NEED TO SPEAK OF GOD'S PURPOSE IN US.

Acting "according to his good purpose" implies we have a personal responsibility about how to act. Our actions need to speak of God's purpose in us. And when our actions are for His purposes, He will know us at that final wedding feast.

MATURE FAITH

Just as are many young children, I was afraid of the dark as a child. To avoid the imagined monsters under my bed I'd take a flying leap onto my bed so my toes didn't even briefly touch the floor beneath the bed. Even with my companion nightlight right next to me, I'd pull the blankets up over my head and snuggle down the mattress far enough so my feet were pinned against the footboard. Yet by the light of day I knew my fears of the dark were the product of my overactive imagination. I was perfectly rational in the light. And now as an adult, I'm perfectly rational about the dark.

I've "grown up." Meaning, what used to scare me, what used to hold me captive, doesn't scare me anymore. I can look at my childhood fears and dismiss them with the wisdom of maturity.

As Christians we need to be growing into mature faith too, because the Lord doesn't want us to remain afraid of the night. The writer of Hebrews laments about fellow Christians who haven't "grown up" in their faith. He complains because they should be chewing on "meat" but are still being spoon-fed milk. "In fact, though by this time you ought to be teachers, you need someone to teach you the elementary truths of God's word all over again. You need milk, not solid food! Anyone who lives on milk, being still an infant, is not acquainted with the teaching about righteousness. But solid food is for the mature, who by constant use have trained themselves to distinguish good from evil" (Hebrews 5:12–14).

Being prepared and being godly means we've given up spoonfuls of milk that are so easy to swallow and have instead progressed to the solid meat of scriptural truths. We can live on the simple "milk" truth that God loves us. Nothing can change that, but there is so much more "meat" on which He wants us to ruminate.

The New Testament redemption story doesn't end with Christ's resurrection. That's just the *beginning*. The rest of the New Testament was written so we would know how to put the redemption story into practice. The rest of the New Testament prepares us for the rest of our lives on earth. It tells us how to conduct ourselves, how to minister to others, and how to live by God's rules and not man's.

> THE REST OF THE NEW TESTAMENT WAS WRITTEN SO WE WOULD KNOW HOW TO PUT THE REDEMPTION STORY INTO PRACTICE.

The only way we can fulfill God's purpose and plan for us individually is by being prepared with the meat of His Word. His Word is called meat because—similar to animal flesh—it has sustaining value. Animal protein feeds us, nourishes us, sustains us. Just as physical meat needs to be ingested to have any nutritional value, so too does God's Word have to be ingested to have any value in our spiritual lives. Jeremiah said, "When your words came, I ate them" (15:16). God's Word feeds us when we are hungry and thirsting for God. It nourishes our love-relationship with Him. And it sustains us when we navigate night watches.

DON'T GROW WEARY

Nothing puts me to sleep quicker than being a passenger in a car at night. The hum of the engine and the lack of anything visually interesting lull me into heavy-eyed silence.

I can relate with the ten virgins who waited for the Bridegroom but finally succumbed to sleep, since I too feel exhausted simply because I'm waiting—whether it's waiting to arrive at a destination or waiting for God to answer my prayer.

Nothing will strain our convictions more than unmet anticipation. We grow tired of waiting. Yet waiting is our walk—sometimes by baby steps—into maturity.

Paul knew that human nature doesn't like to wait. He knew firsthand how it felt to pass time waiting for something to happen (think about how much time he spent in prison). Which is why his words about waiting are so poignant. "Let us not become weary in doing good, for at the proper time we will reap a harvest if we do not give up" (Galatians 6:9). When are crops harvested? When they are grown, when they are ripe and ready to be picked. Paul was saying, "Don't give up during the wait, because the waiting brings the fruit of maturity."

As we grow in this maturity we may not even have a view of the finish line. Like a marathon runner who has miles of pavement to pass under her feet, she can't see the finish line from the starting point, but she knows there is an end point.

So it is with waiting. If we know there is an end point, we can encourage ourselves not to grow tired during the wait. As the five wise virgins knew, the way not to grow weary with discouragement was to be prepared with enough fuel to keep going well into the dark night.

There is a deliberateness to being prepared. Either we ignore the inevitable, like the five foolish virgins, or we acknowledge what is possible and prepare for the unknown.

EXPECTING TO SEE HIM

Look how quickly the disciples forgot what they had just learned in the light on the hill with the five thousand. It took only three night watches—about nine hours—to bring them to a state of fear and discouragement. I'm encouraged to know that even the disciples—the men closest to Christ—were as human as I am!

This was obviously a test—a test of the dark night. The darkness tested them, the wind tested them, the hour tested them, and Christ's apparent abandonment tested them. These tests inquire of our faith: Do you remember in the dark what you know to be true in the light?

Mark's rendition of this same account contributes a little piece of information that adds to the picture. "About the fourth watch of the night [Jesus] went out to them, walking on the lake. *He was about to pass by them . . .*" (Mark 6:48, emphasis added). Why did Jesus nearly pass by them? Because they didn't *see* Him in the dark. Their view was shortsighted: All they saw was the darkness and the hard work, but they had to look beyond their circumstances to see Christ.

Jesus appeared in a place His disciples weren't expecting, so they nearly missed Him. Sounds a bit like us. Let's face it, when we pray we have a certain expectation of how that prayer will be answered. Our way. But often our prayers are answered in a different way, from a different direction, and beyond what we were looking for as an answer.

> HIS ANSWERS TO OUR PRAYERS ALWAYS INCLUDE THE BIGGER PICTURE.

This brings to mind cancer patients who are fervently prayed for to receive healing but who die. Did God ignore the prayers? No, His answer was different than what the intercessors expected. The question is will we accept a different answer than the one *we want*? If our eyes are glued to the only answer we will accept, then we will miss Him. He will pass by us. Not because He doesn't want us to see Him, but because we have to look beyond our limited imaginations. His answers to our prayers always include the bigger picture.

If we feel we've missed the Lord, we can be assured He will appear in a different place. If a person is not healed of an illness and dies, perhaps through his testimony while alive, others will come to know God. Seeds planted during a person's life will break ground in a new place, where we may not have expected. And that's where God is.

THE OFFERED CUP

When we thirst for the things of God will we be selective about the cup He offers us? "I don't like that cup; it's chipped." "That cup is ugly; I won't drink from it." If we choose not to accept what is offered because it is in a different form than we'd like or expected, then we miss God. The cup passes us by and we will find ourselves thirsting for His presence.

The diametrical wisdom of Ecclesiastes says, "When times are good, be happy; but when times are bad, consider: God has made the one as well as the other. Therefore a man cannot discover anything about his future" (7:14). The last line is the clincher, isn't it? Because we are into guesswork and God isn't. We can't know the future, we can't know for certain a dark night watch isn't waiting for us. We certainly can and should rejoice in all the good that God bestows on us every day, and we certainly shouldn't live in fear and dread of what we don't know. Yet this passage reminds us to go with the flow, always remembering God's mighty hand is in the dark as well as the light, and the Light always prevails in the end.

Draw Near to Him:

Dark times are part of living in a day and night world of good versus evil. In what ways can you prepare for dark times in your life? Will you confidently stay prepared for those times when it feels as though Christ is a "long time in coming"? Can you learn to expect to see Him in a different place than how or where you thought He might be?

Drink From His Cup:

" 'Because he loves me,' says the Lord, 'I will rescue him; I will protect him, for he acknowledges my name. He will call upon me and I will answer him; I will be with him in trouble, I will deliver him and honor him' " (Psalm 91:14–15).

CHAPTER ELEVEN

DEEP PASSAGES

M y son and I pedaled our bikes along an off-road trail deeply padded with pine needles. Our tires issued a soft whir as we dodged downed trees and maneuvered around rocks until we came to a narrow footbridge spanning a slow-moving stream. We parked our bikes, and while my son played at the water's edge tossing sticks and rocks into the flowing water, I sat on the bridge. I took off my shoes and socks and dangled my hot feet into the cool stream. Shafts of light split the overhead leaves and streamed down to dapple the water with dark and light patches. One strong shaft of sunlight penetrated clear into the depths of the stream, shining a watery spotlight over a six-foot circle on the sandy bottom. My eyes were naturally drawn to this circle of light as I could see a crayfish scooting around the outer edges and little minnows flitting near the water's surface. Then into the circle of light swam a lone big fish. He cruised along the bottom, moving in and out of the shadow and light. I watched him for a while as he swam effortlessly, seemingly not in a hurry to get anywhere.

Something about the fish intrigued me. Just as tiny air bubbles floated to the surface of the stream, so too did a thought rise to the surface in my consciousness. Big fish swim deep. Little fish swim near the surface. An unbidden prayer rose in my heart: "Lord, I want to be a big fish. I want to swim deep."

I believe this is a desire we all have to get in deep with the Lord. In Calvin Miller's book *Into the Depths of God* (Bethany House, 2000), he writes about how we can be either snorkelers or scuba

> DO WE WANT TO BE
> SURFACE DWELLERS OR
> DEPTH DWELLERS?

divers in our faith. Do we want to be surface dwellers or depth dwellers? Swimming on the surface implies that our perception of God is only a few inches deep. Going deep means we have experienced God's presence at depths we didn't know He or we were capable of.

In the past I've felt discouraged by the even bigger fish I see all around me. I have to remember big fish start small, and I'd rather be a growing fish in God's school than a giant fish who swims alone. All fish drink from the same source. As it is with us, we all are drinking from the same source of the Holy Spirit. The deeper we drink, the more we'll be nourished and the bigger we'll grow.

That's why I want to be a big fish, capable of greater depths. Not a big fish in a little pond, meaning a desire for superiority. But a big fish in a giant expanse of water where I'll never run out of deeper places to go in my love-relationship with the Lord.

There are two parts of the deep things of God. First, we naturally feel uncomfortable in deep places. They are scary. But the second, in a divine juxtaposition, is that we have to go deep to gain the knowledge of who He is. Let's look at both ends of the deep pools to which God is calling us.

OVER OUR HEADS

I grew up sailing with my family. I love boats and I love water. But I've never felt comfortable swimming when I don't know what lies below my feet. I feel particularly unnerved when I know the bottom is hundreds of feet down. Imagined or real threats in the depths keep me from swimming too long or dangling my feet too deep.

I wonder if Jesus' disciples had similar feelings. They loved water, they loved boats, but the wide, open sea, with possible man-eating fish under the surface, might have kept them from diving overboard for a swim.

> WE HAVE TO GO DEEP TO GAIN THE KNOWLEDGE OF WHO HE IS.

When the disciples faced the night of hard rowing and sailing against a hard sea of waves, they certainly knew they were over their heads. Not necessarily literally, but figuratively. They felt abandoned by Jesus, who had briskly sent them on their way without Him after feeding the five thousand. His words and actions confused them. It seems they couldn't understand why He had told them to "go ahead" of Him to a new place. While they sailed and rowed, and the land's edge disappeared, their faith diminished with each passing hour. They were getting in way over their heads for lack of faith and trust.

Theirs was a deep test of trust. Trust that Jesus would meet them at the other side, trust that He was who He said He was. How quickly their faith faltered during the dark night.

Disbelief rocked their boat when they saw what they thought was a ghost. Peter put words to their uncertainty when he said,

"Lord, if it's you, tell me to come to you on the water" (Matthew 14:28). Jesus looked past Peter's impulsive inclinations and answered his challenge with one word: "Come." There is no doubt Jesus knew Peter would deny Him in the not so distant future, so why didn't He just let Peter sink? Because Peter, like us, was worthy of redemption.

This walk-sink-rescue-faith sequence on the water is a foreshadowing of how Peter's faith would play out in the coming days and weeks. He walked in Christ's shadow during their discipling time. He then sank to an all-time low when he denied knowing Jesus right after His arrest. After the Resurrection Jesus rescued Peter from his own despair by giving Peter a final opportunity to follow in His footsteps. And when Peter answered yes to follow Christ away from the only life he'd ever known as a fisherman, it was Peter's final faith walk into a new position of being a fisher of men. The sequence of Peter's life equipped him to become a man who was acquainted with the depths of the Lord.

The deep passages we navigate may have a similar pattern. In our own way, like Peter, we'll say, "If it's really you, prove it!" Jesus may answer and say, "I'd like to prove it, so come." But if we take our eyes off Christ, we will start to sink. Fortunately, the rescue effort is always at Jesus' fingertips. How do we feel about Him after He has us firmly in His grip? Our faith has grown. Not because we walked across the deep passage by ourselves, but because by His loving and strong hand He didn't let us go to a dangerous drowning depth.

DECEIVING DEPTHS

One hot summer day many years ago, while sailing with my parents and sisters, we decided to take a swim as our boat floated by anchor in a little bay on the Massachusetts coast. My mom and one of my sisters dove in while I skeptically eyed the deep green water, contemplating if my desire to cool off was greater than my fear of what swam deeper than my eyesight could penetrate. Just as I decided the risk would be worth the benefit, my mom, who had been peacefully swimming around the boat, screeched, swam hard for the boat ladder, launched herself up the steps, and sprawled across the deck before we could even ask her what was wrong. She breathed hard for a minute, then sheepishly said, "I thought the rudder of the boat was a shark." Perhaps I should mention here that this was the year the thriller movie about a giant, man-eating white shark off Cape Cod—*Jaws*—was released. The power of suggestion is real. The hull and rudder of our boat were indeed a gray color, and with one's imagination it could be mistaken for a giant fish. My mom reacted to a misperception of her mind and eyes before her voice of reason could take over. (And I opted not to swim, after all, that day.)

Reason climbs into the backseat of our minds when a plausible, albeit unlikely, suggestion manhandles our thoughts. Just as my mom was deceived by Hollywood's portrayal of sharks along the Massachusetts coast, so are we often deceived by the possibilities the unknown presents.

The unknown shadowed the disciples' eyes when they saw Jesus walking on the water. The problem was that they didn't recognize Him as Jesus. In terror they thought the shadowy figure on the water was a ghost. Why were they more inclined to believe it was a ghost that approached than Jesus? Why did their minds move more naturally to something evil than something good? Was it because a chunk of their faith and godly reasoning was left in their wake as they moved farther and farther from where they had last seen Christ onshore? Out in the dark night, with a hard wind blowing and the black depths beneath them, they weren't expecting the Master.

They were easily deceived by the power of suggestion in the darkness around them. We too are easily turned aside. Our minds usually follow the closest course of understanding; we don't naturally grasp the divine presence.

This instinct comes to the forefront when we are inexperienced in recognizing deception. Part of the purpose of deep-passage training is to learn to discern deception from truth. Truth is what we need to follow and what will ulti-

PART OF THE PURPOSE OF DEEP-PASSAGE TRAINING IS TO LEARN TO DISCERN DECEPTION FROM TRUTH.

mately lead us into a deeper love-relationship with God and understanding His character.

The apostle Paul felt a deep concern for the young churches of Christ because they seemed to be so vulnerable to deception. In each of his letters, frequently at the beginning, he warns not to be led astray by false teachings or misinterpretations of the gospel of Jesus Christ. His fears must have been justified, because they are prophetic for us even today. We are easily led astray by the power of suggestion or persuasive speaking. Many of the "ghosts" of today's church are false teachings.

When we are called to pass through the deep waters to come to a deeper place of fellowship with Christ, we will be confronted with the ghosts of deception. These untruths shadow our lives in a variety of ways. They can be either personal deception through the lies we tell ourselves in justifying sin, or they can be misleadings with regard to doctrine.

Paul's repeated warnings about false teachings address our

tendency to follow the path of least resistance. We easily follow questionable teaching when deep down we want the falsehood to be true. These shadowed falsehoods require less investment of obedience, usually no death to self, and little or no humility. In fact, shady teachings often promote self, or selfishness, and individual ideas above the Lord's ideals.

Our dance with spiritual deception steps in and out of the dusk in the valley of the shadow of death (see Psalm 23). What is the shadow of death? It's the haunting fear of not only physical death but also spiritual death. If we'd never lived in the light we might not know to be afraid of the dark. But once we have experienced the light, we want it to be a constant part of our lives.

In the previous chapter I spoke of wanting to experience physical darkness by spending a few nights in the cabin my husband had built for me. One late afternoon while at the cabin, before it was dark, I went for a walk deep into the woods and followed a barely discernable deer path to a water hole by the edge of a swamp. As I looked across the swamp to the tall trees lining the perimeter, the sun had just started to drop below the high branches, yet the expanse of reeds and low bushes ahead of me still cast short shadows across each other. For a while I watched birds flitting from stalk to stalk and insects hovering over the bushes. I listened to the quiet and watched the edges of the swamp for bigger wildlife. When the shadows seemed to be reaching away from the sun for a final wave good-bye, I stepped back into the woods and turned to walk to the cabin, about a half-mile away. I hadn't taken more than ten steps into the woods when it suddenly seemed very dark and very still. My mind instinctively turned to all the nocturnal animals that venture out after dusk. Coyotes, porcupines, bear, fox. My strides grew longer and quicker. I had a strong sense of walking through a woods that was not my own. I may have known who owned the land, but no human owned the woods.

I felt as though I had a small taste of walking "through the valley of the shadow of death." Not because I really thought I was going to die, but because I was out after dark. Darkness felt like a threat. I was in the dark, and I knew light felt much more comfortable.

There are always threatening places of darkness within us. The real threat is spiritual darkness. So often the problem is we are blind to the darkness. Our eyes are shut against what we don't know.

Frequently I pray for the Lord to show me where I'm wrong, to open my eyes to my own faults and shortcomings. I don't want to be self-deceived.

Any deception leads us toward the dark valley of spiritual death. As Psalm 23 implies, however, we do need to walk *through* the valleys of shadowy doubt. "Through" implies that light is beckoning from the other end of the valley. The Bible never promises we won't have times of pushing through dark and deep places. It only promises peace at the end. The benefit at the end is worth the risk of the journey.

> WE DO NEED TO WALK THROUGH THE VALLEYS OF SHADOWY DOUBT.

How can we face the shadowy valley, the deep waters, the dark path? The rest of Psalm 23:4 assures us, "You are with me; your rod and your staff, they comfort me." The rod and staff are God's instruments of correction and boundaries and He's within reaching distance to use them, hence the comfort. Just as a shepherd uses these tools to touch his flock or rein them in, keeping them close to him, together, and moving forward through unknown paths, so is God's Word the tool that keeps us on the right path, even through darkness when we can't see clearly the final destination.

PENETRATING THE DEEP

Genesis 1:2 begins, "Darkness was over the surface of the deep, and the Spirit of God was hovering over the waters." In other words, nothing had yet *penetrated* the deep. Darkness was over it, but where was God's Spirit? *Above* the darkness. Darkness existed from the beginning; darkness was all that had penetrated deep, but God's spirit was above it all. And with God's words "Let there be light," there was no longer darkness in the deep places. Forevermore His light would penetrate the deep.

> GOD'S WORD IS ALL ABOUT LIVING IN THE REVELATION OF HIS LIGHT.

When God said across the empty expanse, "Let there be light," He didn't mean only literally, He also meant figuratively. Illumination now covered the expanse and dispelled the dark. Even more, spiritual illumination was given passage into what was about to be created: humankind. God's deeply impacting words could have been "*Let there* be light in people's lives. *Let there* be an avenue by which my Spirit can give light and understanding about me, the great I Am. *Let there* be a desire to walk in the light. *Let there* be a way for women and men to live outside the boundaries of darkness and within the freedom of light."

Every book has an early-on theme sentence, and the Bible's theme couldn't be written more succinctly: "Let there be light."

God's Word is all about living in the revelation of His light. His light is the only thing that can penetrate darkness—the darkness in our hearts and the darkness in our world.

Walking in darkness is like walking around with a blindfold over our eyes. It brings to mind the childhood game Blind Man's Bluff. As the blindfolded person tries to tag the other players, he bumps into walls and furniture and ends the game with bruised shins and knees. It is a simple example of our lives: without light we bump into objects too; they can trip us up and hurt us. Yet all we have to do is to choose to live in the light. Psalm 119:18 requests of the Lord, "Open my eyes that I may see wonderful things in your law." This prayer for revelation could say, "Lord, take my blinders off, remove my blindfold, and let your light be what guides my steps in this giant life-game. I don't want my journey through life to be a precarious one. I want the path to be fully illuminated by the light of your Word."

LIVING IN THE DEEP

Going deep with God is getting into "the know" about Him. Psalm 42:7 says, "Deep calls to deep." A long-held favorite verse, I have pondered its meaning. What "deep" speaks to another "deep"? The deep things of God call to the deep desires in us. Only a deep knowledge of the Lord can speak to the deep needs in us.

ONLY A DEEP KNOWLEDGE OF THE LORD CAN SPEAK TO THE DEEP NEEDS IN US.

Only a clear, mature, deep wisdom of who God is can satisfy our thirst for divine things.

Divine revelation is borne from a serious search of the Scriptures. This was Paul's prayer for the young church in Ephesus: "I keep asking that the God of our Lord Jesus Christ, the glorious Father, may give you the Spirit of wisdom and revelation, so that you may know him better. I pray also that the eyes of your heart may be enlightened in order that you may know the hope to which he has called you, the riches of his glorious inheritance in the saints, and his incomparably great power for us who believe" (Ephesians 1:17–19). Paul had amazing and God-inspired revelation and wisdom, yet one of his greatest prayers was that *all* believers would share in God's knowledge. He didn't want to hoard it for himself; he knew it was to be shared.

THE STAIRS OF RIGHTEOUSNESS

THE CAUSE FOR WHICH WE LIVE AFFECTS EVERYONE WITH WHOM WE COME IN CONTACT.

The Lord wants to bless us with an understanding of Him, His character, how He works, His Word, and His wisdom. Why? The cause and effect of Christianity is simple: the cause for which we live affects everyone with whom we come in contact.

Getting in deep with God is a high calling. It sounds like an oxymoron. Being in a love-relationship with Christ, where more of His wisdom and revelation are imbedded in the depths of who we are, equips us to move "upward" into a life that reflects more of Christ's righteousness in us. "And whatever you do, whether in word or deed, do it all in the name of the Lord Jesus, giving thanks to God the Father through him" (Colossians 3:17). This means whatever we do or speak we are to commit in His name. His ways are higher than ours, and if we are doing something in His name, it should be "higher" also.

Picture this upward life as a giant staircase stepping up into an ever-evolving, ever-growing abiding in God. We gain ground on the stairs with the ingredients of the love-relationship we've been pursuing based on obedience to God's Word. It is, indeed, a high calling. And some of us are afraid of heights. That's why many people set up camp on the same step for their entire lives. They don't want the responsibility of stepping up, of living an upwardly righteous life.

In self-doubt, some others may not feel qualified. Self-doubt is a self-deception; it's a lie we have allowed ourselves to believe. Our qualifier for taking another step upward is simple: We are the chosen children of God. "[Give] thanks to the Father, who has qualified you to share in the inheritance of the saints in the kingdom of light" (Colossians 1:12). Just as my children qualify for any benefits I earn in the work force and any inheritance I may leave upon my death, so too are we qualified to receive from God all that is needed to follow His calling. Nothing *we do* qualifies us. It's our obedience to what *He says to do* that qualifies us. Do you see the difference? The initiation comes from His direction, not our own.

Neither should we make the mistake of thinking that the call on our lives is our own. The prophet Jeremiah said, "I know, O Lord, that a man's life is not his own; it is not for man to direct his steps" (10:23). *The Prayer of Jabez* reveals an underlying theme that deep searchers find appealing. The book challenges Christians to ask for the blessing found in touching other people's lives. What a novel thought! We aren't living our lives for our own benefit but so that others can see God and come into a deeper, personal love-relationship with Him.

Moving up the staircase of righteousness is managed one obedience at a time. We obey the Lord's call, we move up a step closer to God's heart, and we gain a blessing: a heightened view and revelation of who He is.

THE HIGHER WE CLIMB IN EFFECTIVENESS FOR GOD, THE MORE OPEN OUR EYES WILL BE TO THE DEEPER THINGS OF HIM.

It's a visual dichotomy, isn't it? When we go *up* by living a more righteous life, we gain a *deeper* understanding of God. But the higher we climb in effectiveness for God, the more open our eyes will be to the deeper things of Him.

When Jesus challenged Peter to come to Him and walk on the water, Peter may have stepped out of the boat in faith, but he also took a step up in righteousness. Even though he began to sink when his fears distracted him, he didn't lose his foothold on that newly gained step. He came into a new level of understanding of who Christ was. Several days later when Jesus asked Peter, "Who do you say I am?" he confessed wholeheartedly that Christ is the Son of the living God (Matthew 16:15–16). Then Jesus revealed to him the height on the steps of righteousness to which Peter would climb: "And I tell you that you are Peter, and on this rock I will build my church, and the gates of Hades will not overcome it. I will give you the keys of the kingdom of heaven; whatever you bind on earth will be bound in heaven and whatever you loose on earth will be loosed in heaven" (18–19). Jesus was saying, "You've walked across deep waters; you've come into deep revelation of who I am. I am giving you the power and authority to touch people's lives and minister in my name." What is so amazing and humbling for every believer is that even after this prophecy, Peter denied Christ three times (Matthew 26:69–75). Despite this blatant betrayal, God still used Peter to his fullest potential.

This is a solid basis of hope for all of us. Because even as we climb the steps of righteousness, we'll falter, but if our hearts and souls are sincere about wanting to go deep with God, He will lift us up and bring us to new heights, where our thirst for the things of Him can be more readily realized.

Draw Near to Him:

Let's not be afraid to go deep with God. Though we may at times feel as if we are grasping for air and understanding, He will be faithful to keep us by His side. There, within reaching distance of His Almighty hand, we will learn to recognize Him, understand Him, and be with Him at a new level.

Drink From His Cup:

"[We] must keep hold of the deep truths of the faith with a clear conscience" (1 Timothy 3:9).

CHAPTER TWELVE

STEADFASTNESS

The devil aims high. His personal standards may be low, but he knows hitting high has a domino effect that can level whole groups of God's people. On the stairs of righteousness his marksmanship targets the highest steps, the places where Christian leaders and deeply committed people dwell. The crosshairs of his weapon sights are aimed at our individual hearts and minds. If he can pierce these inner places, the soul takes a blow. Then he sits back and watches us suffer.

If we know he aims high, are we to duck to avoid his arrows? No, we are told to stand firm and resist. This is why Paul instructed the Ephesians with a word picture of how to don the full armor of God (6:10–18). And as Bible teachers have noted, there's no armor protecting the backside of the target in these verses. This is because when we are climbing the stairs of righteousness we face life's trials head-on.

There are two certainties in our Christian journey: We have an assured home of eternal life in heaven; and en route we will face attack. We can be sure the devil's hazards are meant to discourage us.

The devil is against us. Against our faith, against our preaching the Gospel, against the hope we profess in Christ, against the daily joy and peace in which we live, against our love-relationship with the Lord.

We're not alone in this experience of finding ourselves pitted against the devil. The disciples knew this feeling too. As they tried to row and sail across the expanse of water as Jesus told them to, they hit a wall of exhaustion, doubt, and fear, all wrapped up in the words: "The boat was already a considerable distance from land, buffeted by the waves because the wind was against it" (Matthew 14:24).

The wind was *against* them: pushing hard against their best efforts. Yet their arms labored in an effort to be obedient to what Jesus had told them to do: go to the other side. But the wind itself was set against their obedience.

Don't we too find ourselves working hard toward something the Lord told us to do, yet find that circumstances seem to be set against us? But if we could reach the destination of the "other side" on our own, wouldn't that devalue His direction? If we could row against and through the hard wind and waters on our own, we would never experience His amazing faithfulness. We'd be robbed of the profound sense of God's provision and protection.

> IF WE COULD ROW AGAINST AND THROUGH THE HARD WIND AND WATERS ON OUR OWN, WE WOULD NEVER EXPERIENCE HIS AMAZING FAITHFULNESS.

LIVING IN GOD-CONFIDENCE

God wants us to be aware of our finiteness so we have a sense of need for Him. He wants us to know there is something *against* us so we have a greater sense of need for something that is *for* us. He wants to see us succeed. He wants to see us come through those obstacles that are against us. Why? These hard places grow our confidence in our faith in Him. Not self-confidence, but God-confidence.

At the beginning of this book we talked about standing at the crossroads of Need and Will. Thirst for the things of God brought us to this crossroad. This has been a journey of seeing your need, accepting that you have a need, and then asking God to fill the need. Don't deny His meeting your need at this last crossing! Talk of the devil being against us can be frightening. Yet we can't turn our backs in defeat. It's steadfastness that keeps us dipping our oars a little harder and a little deeper and a little more stubbornly to get through what has been set against us.

Steadfastness and faith are marriage partners. Hand in hand they support one another. Faith is a noun but it is also an action. Because faith is unseen, we need to develop a doable action to profess it. That's what steadfastness is. The disciples' faith in Christ wasn't with them for most of the hard row across the open water, but steadfastness made them keep on keeping on. Author and speaker Joyce Meyer admonishes, "Keep doing the last thing God told you to do until He tells you to do something else."

STUBBORN OBEDIENCE

God's request of us to obey might not be called obedience if we were always willing to do what He asks. Being obedient to what God wants us to do often goes against our fleshly nature. We want what we want, when we want it, and now. Maybe the disciples would have liked to stop rowing against the hard waves and just let the wind and water carry them. But this would have meant being disobedient and giving up. Jesus told them to cross over to the other side. He didn't offer them a second option.

He doesn't offer us a second option either. We have to live for the Lord, or we're choosing to live against Him. We can't have it both ways. We don't teach our children to obey us only half the time—

> WE HAVE TO LIVE FOR THE LORD, OR WE'RE CHOOSING TO LIVE AGAINST HIM.

when it's convenient for them or when they want to. Neither does the Lord allow us half-obedience.

Half-obedience indicates we believe in only part of how the Lord instructs us to live. Why does He instruct us? Because He is God! He indisputably knows best. We either believe this or we don't.

Have you ever bought something that required assembly? We should know to steer clear of any product that provides "easy step-by-step" instructions. But the glossy picture on the outside of the box looks so simple and perfect that we decide we can do it. What if you were to open the box and begin to assemble the item, but halfway through you decided to ignore the rest of the instructions? Pieces would end up attached in the wrong places, the instruction sheet would be smeared with glue, and it would take twice as long to assemble as you thought it would. You would wish you'd never started the project in the first place and that you'd listened to the salesman who offered to assemble it for an extra twenty dollars!

Why do we intentionally frustrate ourselves?

Yet this is exactly what we do when we are trying to live more closely to God's Word. Too often we hamstring ourselves with poor choices or disobedience.

Wanting the Lord to quench our thirst for the things of God means we need to abide in Him and with Him. We need to be close to Him, to set our faces like flint against adversity (Isaiah 50:7). We must live daily in His presence, because frustration lives outside His presence.

It seems David thought along these same lines of wanting to ascend the stairs of righteousness and leave frustration behind so he could be closer to God's heart. David was a contemplator. How often he asks himself a question, then goes on to answer it. He was one of God's chosen instruction writers for this thing we call life. He offers us assembly notes that, if we follow them, will lead us upward and away from the very frustrations that proved to be his own learning curve.

> Lord, who may dwell in your sanctuary?
> Who may live on your holy hill?
> He whose walk is blameless
> and who does what is righteous,
> who speaks the truth from his heart
> and has no slander on his tongue,
> who does his neighbor no wrong
> and casts no slur on his fellowman,
> who despises a vile man
> but honors those who fear the Lord,
> who keeps his oath even when it hurts,
> who lends his money without usury
> and does not accept a bribe against the innocent.
> He who does these things will never be shaken. (Psalm 15)

This is a tall order. But it makes so much sense. We can paraphrase it "Be good, do good." A user-friendly promise follows these stiff instructions. "He who does these things will never be shaken." Why will we not be shaken? Because the more we identify with the righteousness of God in our lives the stronger we will be to stand firm. Just as at the site of a broken bone new and dense bone grows, so too at the point of hardship in our lives new strength grows.

Believe me, I've felt the tremors underfoot when my world threatens me with a hard shaking. I don't live in the land of Shangri-La, eyeing the sights through rose-colored glasses. In the three months following September 11, 2001, like so many other people, my world felt like it had taken a sharp left-hand turn. In early October, on my birthday, I was in a serious head-on car collision that left me with nerve damage in my right arm. Several weeks later I endured a two-week debilitating virus. Around the same time my husband and I found out our medical insurance would cover only half of a several-thousand-dollar medical expense for our son. Then I received a dishearteningly low royalty check from the sales of one of my books. In the midst of all this I learned a dear friend had breast cancer. And finally, just a few weeks before Christmas, my father was diagnosed with a benign brain tumor, requiring surgery. The ground under my feet suddenly felt suspiciously tremulous.

The devil had taken aim right at my heart and mind. He hit me physically and emotionally through the people I love the most. Yet what the devil intended to weaken in me only served to do the opposite.

There is a psychological term used for the behavior of young people who say or act in opposition to what they've been told. It's called "oppositional." You say "black," they say "white." You say "yes," they say "no." Those are the same maddening rapid responses of the devil. He acts the opposite of what God says and does. His intent is to anger, frustrate, and weaken us. But if he is oppositional to me, I'm stubbornly oppositional right back at him.

All these difficult circumstances in such a short time only served to strengthen my stubborn conviction to stay tight with God. I knew I had no hope without Him. Through the devil's smoke screens I had a clarity of God's sovereignty that only grew stronger after each devilish attack. Though emotionally I felt as pockmarked as Swiss cheese, my vision became clearer.

Fanny Crosby, writer of hundreds of hymns and praise songs, experienced a heart love, knew a big beautiful God, and spoke of Him with eloquence. She was also blind. She lived on God's holy hill, impervious to any shaky ground. She knew even if her own body was set against her, her spirit rejoiced in the One who was always *for* her.

GOD WILL NOT FORSAKE US.

HE CANNOT FORSAKE

HIS OWN.

We too can know the joy that comes with unshakable confidence in God's faithfulness. David proclaimed, "I have never seen the righteous forsaken." God will not forsake us. He cannot forsake His own. He's had ample opportunity, but He won't turn His back on us. His steadfast love for us is what steadies the ground under us. The assurance of His faithfulness is the hope we hold on to when tremblers strike at our heart. Because of God's faithfulness we can stand steadfast. Fast and steady and ready to face *anything*.

GET IN THE ZONE

Hard and true sports people all confess to the same phenomenon when they've reached the last reserve or physical resource in competition. An unseen switch opens a floodgate and suddenly an unknown and internal power carries them through to the end. It's part mental, part physical, part metaphysical reserve that overrides any conscious thought on the athlete's part. It just happens. They may not be able to make it happen, but they know it will happen. In this zone all external distractions and all inner warning signals have been tuned out, and tunnel vision of the end result is what drives them on.

Christians who live in a similar "zone" have tunnel vision for nothing but what the Lord wants. This doesn't mean we ignore daily responsibilities, but it means we take the adversarial nature of the devil in stride. He can't distract us because it's outside of the vision God has set before us. The devil can't stand against the power we have in the one and only God Almighty. Christ's name alone is the banner of victory we carry on our march toward heaven. As Peter proclaimed from his own shame-healed heart, "And the God of all grace, who called you to his eternal glory in Christ, after you have suffered a little while, will himself restore you and make you strong, firm and steadfast. To him be the power for ever and ever. Amen" (1 Peter 5:10–11).

GOD IS GOOD ... ALL THE TIME

The more we don't know, the more we do know we need God. Know Him as the good God that He is.

Depression is a genetic inheritance I've learned to live with. I can so easily look down that slippery path and dangle a foot precipitously close. But in wanting to break this tendency, I tried an experiment. The experiment has been so successful I continue to do it. Each morning when I wake up, even before I think about how cluttered my calendar is with "to-do's," I lift my praise:

"Lord, you are a good God." I don't pray for strength; I don't pray for a bright, sunny, clear day; I don't even pray for wisdom—all those requests may come later. I know His character is good, and I want my day to start by professing this heart truth. The result of this sincere prayer has changed my life. A bubbling sense of anticipation brings me to full wakefulness. I then go through my day with an amazing joy and excitement about what God is going to do. But even more remarkable, I may lay my head down on the same pillow where I began my day sixteen hours before, and though nothing circumstantially exciting may have happened, I will feel as though God was indeed good to me all day: He fed me that abiding joy all day; He gave me another day to be thankful for His goodness; He was faithful to His Word: "With joy you will draw water from the wells of salvation" (Isaiah 12:3).

> WHEN WE PROCLAIM THE
> GOOD CHARACTER OF GOD,
> WE OPEN OUR SOULS
> TO EXPERIENCE IT.

When we proclaim the good character of God, we open our souls to experience it. Our mouths and minds are the gateways to our hearts and souls. What starts as a confession about the Truth from our mouths becomes an unshakable Truth in our spirits.

WHAT GOD WANTS

It's a little frightening to put down in ink what I believe God wants. How can I possibly know what the Lord of the universe wants? But because I am confident in His love for you and me as individuals, and because I have faith in His character, I trust these words are true.

God wants you. All of you. He wants your heart, soul, mind, and strength. He wants your pain; He wants your joy. He wants your fears; He wants your confidences. He wants your hopes; He wants your failures. He wants your love; He wants your anger. He wants your faith; He wants your insecurities. He wants you where you are, not where you've been. He wants you to be steadfast in your conviction that He is and was and will forever be a good God. He wants you to know Him, experience Him, love Him, cherish Him, obey Him, serve Him, and be at peace with Him.

Above all, He wants your thirst for Him met through a love-relationship with Him. He wants to hold out a dripping, overflowing, sweet, and refreshing cup of His uncontainable goodness to be the only source of Life on which you live.

Take and drink.

Draw Near to Him:

God's goodness defeats the devil's "against us" nature. Defeat is not an option in the marriage partnership of faith and steadfastness. In what ways can you make a choice to stay steadfast in your newly gained ground?

Drink From His Cup:

"He said to me: 'I am the Alpha and the Omega, the Beginning and the End. To him who is thirsty I will give to drink without cost from the spring of the water of life. He who overcomes will inherit all this, and I will be his God and he will be my son'" (Revelation 21:6–7).

Discover Peace,
Discover God

Too often today we think of personal retreat as a chance to run away from something—hectic schedules, work deadlines, demanding family responsibilities—rather than the wonderful opportunity to run *to* our Creator and Lord. *Quiet Places* answers our yearnings for a deeper relationship with God, offering thought-provoking, spirit-prodding inspiration that will help you as a modern woman face issues of stress, forgiveness, loss, relationships, and more. Author Jane Rubietta's moving narrative-style writing and carefully selected meditative Scriptures will encourage you to seize the chance to be led to the Savior. Bring your Bible, and slip away for a time in *Quiet Places*.